Wetlands

An Introduction to Ecology, the Law, and Permitting

Theda Braddock

with contributions from
L. Reed Huppman

 Government Institutes, Inc. • Rockville, Maryland

Government Institutes, Inc., 4 Research Place, Suite 200,
Rockville, Maryland 20850

ISBN: 0-86587-467-0

Printed in the United States of America

TABLE OF CONTENTS

ABOUT THE AUTHORS

Theda Braddock is an attorney with the Washington, D.C. firm of Freer & McGarry, a Professional Corporation, in its Greenbelt, Maryland office where she practices environmental, land use, and securities law. She is a member of the California, Maryland, and Massachusetts Bars. She advises developers, private individuals, consultants, and conservation foundations on wetland and other environmental issues with an emphasis on mediated settlement, although she is no stranger to Federal Court. When not practicing law, she lives in Annapolis, Maryland with her husband, Richard P. Cox, and two children, Theda (the Fourth!) and Edward.

L. Reed Huppman is a geomorphologist and plant ecologist with over 17 years of experience working in wetlands in the U.S. and abroad. He holds degrees in geology, geomorpology, and ecology. He has been extensively involved in the restoration design and construction of stream and wetlands and has received the U.S. Army Corps of Engineers Honor Award for Environmental Design as well as the Chesapeake Bay Program's Habitat Restoration Award for the Kenilworth Marsh Restoration project on the Anacostia River in Washington, D.C.. Mr. Huppman is a senior environmental scientist with EA Engineering, Science, and Technology, Inc., in Hunt Valley, Maryland, ouside of Baltimore.

INTRODUCTION

When we planned this book, we hoped to create a text which would be useful to wetland scientists and real estate developers, and to the attorneys for both sides. Although there are very few laws which bring such a disparate group of people together, the Clean Water Act is such a law. In recent years it has become a polarizing issue, particularly as the public's knowledge of the functions of wetlands becomes more widespread, but the need for housing continues to increase.

Recently, real estate developers have turned their eye on wetlands as developable land. And far from being the dark, odorous miasmas breeding disease they were once thought to be,[1] wetlands are now recognized as an important, vital natural resource in their own right as well as a supplier to many other environmental systems. The basic question becomes whether we should allow all wetlands to be filled in, which was the official government policy a century ago, or should we protect this dwindling resource at the expense of other important societal goals? This book tries to take the middle ground—that development is necessary, but it can be conducted in a reasoned manner so that both sides are served. Perhaps there will be less unproductive dissension if the real estate developer understands the process and complexities of the scientist's effort to define and delineate a wetland, and if the scientist and the environmentalist understand the difficulties the courts have had in melding traditional concepts of the property rights of individual landowners with environmental science and the public good.

As we considered how to explain our position to two groups in traditional opposition to each other, we thought it might be helpful to explain the science and the law in terms that both sides could understand. Thus, after a short exposition of the political side of wetland regulation in Chapter 1, we have followed with a chapter on basic wetland science, explaining what wetlands are, how they fit into the complex natural scheme, and what the particular functions and values are of wetlands

---

[1] Wetlands were even dubbed "nuisances". *Leovy v. United States*, 177 U.S. 621, 44 L.Ed. 914, 20 S.Ct. 797 (1900); See also 72 ALR 2d 554, §1.

themselves. Chapter 3 discusses the scientific classification of wetlands. In the next chapter we describe how wetlands are delineated, which has been the source of much confusion and hard feeling between the two groups. Following that description, we added a chapter about §404 permits, including a description of the permit requirement, the activities which require a permit, those activities which are exempt, and, finally, a description of nationwide and general permits. The next chapter describes the permit process itself, and then, how the permits will be enforced through enforcement procedures and administrative penalties. The final chapter describes litigation and defenses under the Clean Water Act.

Attempting to write a definitive text in the midst of the current turmoil has been less than easy. Indeed, the future of wetland regulation is uncertain due to the various agendas of the conflicting interests. Nonetheless, we hope that this text will somehow contribute to an ultimate agreement on a method of delineating wetlands so as to allow regulation of activities in them in a manner which comports with wetland science and the law fairly, one which allows all parties to concentrate their efforts on intelligent development and rational science. The controversy can only be resolved by a fuller understanding of the positions of landowners, wetland scientists, attorneys, and environmentalists on both sides of the fence.

Even though we have tried to give our readers a clear understanding of the Clean Water Act, it is equally important to recognize that wetlands are only part of the vast aquatic ecosystem, and that the Clean Water Act is only a fairly recent expression of legal doctrines, some of which are thousands of years old, and some of which are unique to recent American jurisprudence.

CHAPTER ONE
POLITICAL PERSPECTIVES

One basic American concept which is extremely relevant to understanding the Clean Water Act is the source of power by which the federal government regulates water at all. Article I, §8, Clause 3 of the United States Constitution, the "Commerce Clause", requires that before the federal government can regulate an activity, it must have an effect on interstate commerce. The Commerce Clause is broadly construed because so many activities either have an actual, immediate effect of interstate commerce, or might have an effect.[2] Indeed, the Commerce Clause was the original source of authority for such diverse federal laws as the original civil rights legislation because racial segregation has an effect on interstate commerce. The federal authority under the Commerce Clause for the Corps's assertion of jurisdiction over wetlands can be found in the words of §404 itself in which the use, destruction, or degradation of wetlands "could affect interstate commerce".[3]

Another basic jurisdictional concept is water law. Originally this particular legal system dealt exclusively with *quantities* of water (whereas the Clean Water Act, by its very title, deals with water *quality*) by allocating it among various users according to various standards of fairness. Since most of the water was clean, regulating pollution was not a problem. However, as more people used more water, in addition to water shortages, water pollution became an issue requiring legislation. It does not matter how

---

[2] But see *U.S. v. Lopez*, № 93-1260, a U.S. Supreme Court case decided April 26, 1995, which appeared to cut back on the government's broad assertion of authority under the Commerce Clause to forbid individuals from possessing a firearm in school zones, stating that such an assertion of power would "convert congressional authority under the Commerce Clause to a general police power".

[3] See also *Hoffman Homes, Inc. v. EPA*, 999 F.2d 256 (7th Cir. Ill. 1993), upholding the concept that a "potential" effect on interstate commerce was sufficient for purposes of Clean Water Act jurisdiction, but denying jurisdiction on other grounds.

much water there is if it was so polluted that none of it could be used. Stated otherwise, water law assumes the existence of clean water in allocating quantities of water to competing users. But the Clean Water Act, a water quality law, was enacted as the logical offspring of water use law when sufficient quantities of clean water began to dwindle. This text focusses on the federal Clean Water Act, with discussion of another historic source of U.S. Army Corps of Engineers jurisdiction, the Rivers and Harbors Act of 1899, where relevant. Two other statutes occasionally come into play, the National Environmental Policy Act and the "Swampbuster" provision of the 1985 Farm Bill, as do three additional agencies: the U.S. Environmental Protection Agency, the U.S. Fish and Wildlife Service, and the Soil Conservation Service of the U.S. Department of Agriculture, under their own particular authorizing statutes.

Although the Clean Water Act is now over twenty years old, its future is far from clear just as its history has been one of almost constant disagreement and lawsuits. Originally there were four definitions of wetlands used by the four agencies involved. The U.S. Army Corps of Engineers had its own manual for delineating wetlands, the 1987 *Corps of Engineers Wetlands Delineation Manual.* Then the four agencies agreed on the 1989 *Federal Manual for Identifying and Delineating Jurisdictional Wetlands,* which was used until late 1991, when its use was prohibited unless the landowners consented to its use[4] while the agencies considered comments from a new document, the *Proposed Revisions.*[5]

Instead, Congress intervened again and insisted that the National Academy of Sciences prepare a report on the delineation of wetlands. As of the date of this writing, the panel of the National Academy of Sciences which is to write the report, without which there will be no new delineation Manual, has not completed the task to which

---

[4]   See the "Johnson Amendment" to the Energy and Water Development Appropriations Act of 1992, Pub.L. № 102-104, 105 Stat. 510 (1991) and the Energy and Water Development Appropriations Act of 1993, Pub.L.№ 102-377, 106 Stat. 1315 (1992).

[5]   56 Fed.Reg. 40446 (1991).

it had been appointed by President Clinton. The Academy's report is expected in May, 1995.

Meanwhile, a number of bills have been introduced in Congress. These bills propose a number of changes to the Clean Water Act, including time limitations on permit application consideration by the U.S. Army Corps of Engineers, consideration to be given to landowners for compensation when their land is regulated to varying degrees, new guidelines which provide that a review of alternative activities proposed by a permit applicant must be commensurate with the severity of the impact and take into consideration the functions and values of the impacted wetland to the watershed in which it is located, the establishment of mitigation banks,[6] certification of federal wetland delineators, and a possible end to U.S. Army Corps of Engineers and Environmental Protection Agency involvement in wetland regulatory programs which have been "assumed" by individual states.[7]

---

[6]   On March 6, 1995, the U.S. Army Corps of Engineers, Environmental Protection Agency, the Natural Resources Conservation Service of the Department of Agriculture, the Fish and Wildlife Service of the Department of the Interior, and the National Oceanic and Atmospheric Administration of the Department of Commerce jointly issued proposed guidance regarding the establishment, use, and operation of mitigation banks for the purpose of providing compensatory mitigation for permitted adverse impacts to wetlands under authority of §404 of the Clean Water Act and the "Swampbuster provision" of the Food Security Act. 60 Fed.Reg. 12286-12293.

[7]   See also *Friends of the Crystal River v. EPA*, 794 F.Supp. 674 (W.D.Mich. 1992), *aff'd.* 35 F.3d 1073 (6th Cir. 1994); 46 ALR 3d 1422, Supp. §14.

CHAPTER TWO
ECOLOGICAL PERSPECTIVES

From an ecological perspective, wetlands have long been described as transition or intermediate zones between terrestrial and aquatic ecosystems. Wetlands share attributes of both systems but are clearly unique ecosystems. Wetlands occur in an almost infinite variety of type, size, and location depending on a range of environmental factors including climate, topography, geology, landscape history, and hydrology. The latter, however, is the primary environmental factor controlling the existence and extent of wetlands. In a simplistic sense, if there is too little water the system is upland; if there is too much water the system is aquatic or deepwater habitat. Changes in hydrology can alter wetlands to uplands and vice versa. The hydrology which creates wetlands also creates unique environmental conditions such as saturated soils where various biogeochemical reactions and transformations take place. This view presents three important concepts regarding wetlands:

1. Wetlands are part of the ecological continuum or gradient between aquatic and terrestrial ecosystems;

2. Due to their transitional niche in the landscape, wetlands provide a unique niche for various and complex biological and geochemical processes which can directly or indirectly benefit terrestrial and aquatic ecosystems; and

3. The nature and extent of a given wetland varies spatially and temporally depending on the supply of water, which is often variable and dynamic.

These characteristics have made the definition and delineation of wetlands difficult, controversial, and vital. However, Man's systems for categorizing nature are often arbitrary, and few aspects of the natural landscape exhibit clear or precise boundaries. More often a system changes gradually over an environmental gradient or continuum, and it is often in boundary conditions that the great complexities of natural systems are most apparent. But, in order to manage and regulate wetlands, legal definition and delineation are necessary.

WETLAND DEFINITIONS

The search for a clear definition of wetlands has evolved over the last forty years. Given the transitional nature of wetlands between upland and aquatic environments, the problems in definition are greatest at these boundaries. This is further complicated in many nontidal wetlands by seasonal and longer cycle variability in hydrology due to precipitation patterns and other climatic effects. Lastly, there is enormous geographic variation in wetlands reflecting differences in climate, geohydrology, and plant communities.

Consequently, wetland definitions often reflect the purpose for which they were developed. Earlier definitions were developed primarily for descriptive and/or classification purposes which could facilitate inventory and research. In the last decade, the need for a legally binding and scientifically defensible definition has become critical as the battle over wetland protection and regulation has escalated.

Circular 39

An early wetland definition was developed by the U.S. Fish and Wildlife Service for the purposes of wetland inventory in 1956. This publication, *Wetlands of the United*

States, Their Extent and Value for Waterfowl and Other Wildlife, is better known by its government document designation, Circular 39. The definition was:

> The term "wetlands". . . refers to lowlands covered with shallow and sometimes temporary or intermittent waters. They are referred to by such names as marshes, swamps, bogs, wet meadows, potholes, sloughs, and river-overflow lands. Shallow lakes and ponds, usually with emergent vegetation as a conspicuous feature, are included in the definition, but the permanent waters of streams, reservoirs, and deep water lakes are not included. Neither are water areas that are so temporary as to have little or no effect on the development of moist soil vegetation.

The Circular 39 definition clearly places wetlands between upland and aquatic environments, however this system biased towards waterfowl habitat and therefore the larger and wetter end of the wetland spectrum or continuum. Smaller, isolated or topographically higher wetlands such as spring seeps or fens, would not necessarily fit within the resolution of this definition. Nevertheless, this definition was effective for this early inventory of U.S. wetlands, and it has served as the primary basis for subsequent wetland definitions.

Canadian Definition

Developed in 1979 for the purposes of wetland inventory, this definition is significant because of the emphasis on a range of hydrologic regimes, wetland or hydric soils, and the biogeochemical processes characteristic of wetlands (Tarnocai 1979):

> Wetland is defined as land having the water table at, near, or above the land surface or which is saturated for a long enough period to promote wetland or aquatic processes as indicated by hydric soils, hydrophytic vegetation, and various kinds of biological activity which are adapted to the wet environment.

Cowardin Definition

The U.S. Fish and Wildlife Service published a new wetland definition in the *Classification of Wetlands and Deepwater Habitats of the United States* (Cowardin et al., 1979). This definition and classification system served as the basis for the National Wetland Inventory which has been administered by the U.S. Fish and Wildlife Service. The inventory is based on interpretation of color infrared aerial photography at 1:60,000 scale. This mapping program is enormous in scope and not yet complete. Approximately 80% of the conterminous United States, 26% of Alaska, and all of Hawaii and the U.S. Territories have been mapped (USFWS 1994). The U.S. Fish and Wildlife Service is mandated to complete the mapping of the lower 48 states by 1998 and Alaska by the year 2000. The Cowardin system definition was developed by an interdisciplinary team of biologists, ecologists, and geologists and is broad in scope:

> Wetlands are lands transitional between terrestrial and aquatic systems where the water table is usually at or near the surface or the land is covered by shallow water. . .Wetlands must have one or more of the following three attributes: (1) at least periodically, the land supports predominantly hydrophytes, (2) the substrate is predominantly undrained hydric soil, and (3) the substrate is nonsoil and is saturated with water or covered by shallow water at some time during the growing season of each year.

This definition is significant because it is very comprehensive in that it includes areas which would otherwise be considered aquatic habitats. In addition it introduces a three parameter approach but requires that only one of the three parameters be met. The Cowardin system is the most widely accepted descriptive system for wetlands in the United States. The system is discussed in more detail in Chapter 3.

Regulatory Definitions

The definitions above were developed for inventory purposes. They are not suitable for legally defining the boundaries of an individual wetland in the field for regulatory control. In order to regulate dredge and fill permits under §404 of the 1977 Clean Water Act, a more concise definition was required.

In the United States, wetlands are currently defined by the U.S. Army Corps of Engineers (Federal Register 1982) and the U.S. Environmental Protection Agency (Federal Register 1980) as:

> Those areas that are inundated or saturated by surface or ground water at a frequency and duration sufficient to support, and that under normal circumstances do support, a prevalence of vegetation typically adapted for life in saturated soil conditions. Wetlands generally include swamps, marshes, bogs, and similar areas.

This definition serves as the basis for the *1987 Corps of Engineers Wetland Delineation Manual* which defines wetlands through a field investigative methodology requiring the presence of three wetland parameters: hydrology, hydric soils, and hydrophytic vegetation. The 1987 Manual draws a clear distinction between a technical guideline for wetland determination in the field and the Cowardin system for wetland classification. The 1987 Manual is also clearly more restrictive than the Cowardin system, requiring all three of the parameters to be present whereas the Cowardin system requires only one. This definition and methodology are discussed in more detail in Chapter 4, Wetland Delineation.

THE REALITY OF WETLANDS IN THE FIELD

The evolution of the wetland definition demonstrates an increasing refinement necessary for legal and regulatory purposes. And the current definition seems concise and reasonable in print. But how does this definition translate to the myriad types and great complexity of real wetlands in the landscape? Furthermore, how can we begin to assess the relative importance of an individual wetland in one setting versus another? These are some of the issues challenging wetland science today.

On a macroscopic geographic scale, wetlands occur in great variety and geographical range: from above timberline to below sea level, from rain forest to desert, and from arctic to tropical environments. Estimates have put the extent of wetlands worldwide at 6.4% of the total land area of the planet. As one would expect, the greatest areas of wetlands occur in the humid regions of the globe **(Table 2.1)**.

Table 2.1. Concentration of Wetlands Areas.

Estimates have put the extent of wetlands wordwide at 6.4% of the total area of the planet. As one would expect, the greatest areas of wetlands occur in the humid regions of the globe. There are an estimated 6.5 million square kilometers of wetlands in the humid regions (boreal, sub-boreal, subtropical, and tropical) versus 1.9 million square kilometers in the semiarid and arid regions of the earth. The boreal and tropical regions support the greatest areas of wetlands with an estimated 2.6 and 2.64 million square kilometers respectively. There are an estimated 1.0 million square kilometers of sub-boreal wetlands and 2.1 million square kilometers of subtropical wetlands (Mitsch and Gosselink, 1984).

In some situations wetlands constitute entire regions: the Everglades of the southern third of the Florida peninsula, the Mississippi River delta which comprises much of Louisiana and the Mississippi alluvial plain which extends northward to Missouri; the estuarine, tidal wetlands of the Mid-Atlantic; the vast northern peatlands of North America and Eurasia; the Amazon basin which comprises and area approximately two-thirds the size of the U.S.; the Camargue region of France which is the delta of the Rhone River. From a geological perspective, the vast coal beds of the Carboniferous period represent ancient wetland deposits of enormous extent which existed for millions of years.

Wetlands are also integral components of the predominantly upland regions of the world and can occur virtually anywhere in the gradient or landscape continuum from terrestrial to aquatic ecosystems. Small spring or seep wetlands can occur high on hillsides, in headwater drainage swales, or at the foot of slopes. Riparian bottomland or floodplain wetlands occupy valley floors and may extend for many miles along rivers and streams. Inland freshwater marshes occur as hydrologically isolated basins, in the channels of low gradient rivers, or peripheral to natural lakes and ponds or man made reservoirs where they often occur on alluvial bars or deltas where rivers discharge their loads.

WETLAND FUNCTIONS AND VALUES

Wetlands have traditionally been valued for their fish and wildlife habitat attributes. Tidal wetlands and the adjacent tidewaters have long been productive fishing grounds for shell and fin fish, and hunters have known for millennia that wetlands are the prime hunting grounds for waterfowl and many fur bearers. In fact prior to the promulgation of the Clean Water Act, the majority of the wetlands protected in the U.S. during this century were purchased by the U.S. Fish and Wildlife Service or state fish and game agencies because of their importance as breeding, migratory, and/or wintering grounds for game species. Most of the U.S. Fish and Wildlife Refuge system is still managed primarily for game species, but these areas have also provided important refuge for numerous other non-game species as well. The management focus of the National Wildlife Refuge system is beginning to shift as public interest has grown in passive enjoyment of wildlife and natural areas (i.e., birding and environmental education). But the hunting industry still supports a significant portion of the federal and state wildlife refuge programs and the wetlands they protect through the duck stamp/hunting permit program.

Additional wetland values to society have been recognized in recent decades. These values are primarily related to water quality and quantity effects which result from the natural functions of many wetland systems. The list of these functions and values has become somewhat institutionalized and is often attributed generically to all wetlands across the board. Wetlands, however, are extremely diverse and variable, and not all wetlands are created equal. It is probably safe to say that no individual wetland is capable of providing all of the standard functions and values attributed to wetlands. Furthermore, many of the functions wetlands perform are complex and not that well understood. This is due in part to the great variety of wetlands and the relative youthfulness of wetland science but also to the complex interactions of biological and geochemical processes at work in wetlands. Investigation of wetland functions requires a true interdisciplinary scientific approach to unravel the interplay of natural processes at work.

The standard "functions and values" frequently attributed to wetlands are described briefly below and in greater detail in the following section on the wetland processes.

Water Quality: Wetlands are often described metaphorically as the "kidneys of the landscape" because many wetland studies have demonstrated their capability to cleanse water through biogeochemical transformation of various pollutants, particularly nutrients. Wetlands can also function as "sinks" which retain pollutants. However, research has also demonstrated that the beneficial water quality properties of wetlands are extremely complex and variable within and between individual wetlands and wetland systems and are dependent on environmental factors such as hydrology, season, position in the landscape, soils, and geology. While some wetlands have been clearly shown to be sinks for nutrients, others are net exporters of nutrients. Or, a given wetland may be a net sink during one season and a net exporter in another. Research has suggested that in a given drainage basin, the topographic positions of individual wetlands may strongly influence cleansing functions (Whigam, et al., 1988). Small

12

riparian wetlands adjacent to headwater streams have been shown to be more effective in removing nitrogen and coarse soil particles while bottomland wetlands were more effective in removing fine sediment particles and attached phosphorous.

Flood Attenuation: Wetlands are also described as "sponges" which absorb water during rain or flooding. However, since wetlands are usually saturated with water their capacity to absorb additional water is limited. The ability to trap or hold floodwaters is primarily a topographic phenomenon, i.e., wetlands often occupy depressions. This function is strongly influenced by position in the landscape. Riparian bottomland hardwood and floodplain wetlands probably have the greatest flood attenuation effects due primarily to their position in the landscape. They can store and attenuate flood waters when streams or rivers overflow their banks. Unaltered, natural floodplains provide this function with or without vegetation, but the presence of vegetation and forests in particular can enhance this function through the creation of great roughness or friction which can slow floodwater velocities, and to a lesser extent through transpiration which, during the growing season, can pump significant quantities of subsurface water through the trees and into the atmosphere. Small wetlands in headwater drainage swales and streams can have the same effects on a smaller scale and retard and attenuate the delivery of upland runoff to downstream waters. Depressional wetlands can also store significant quantities of surface runoff during rain events but again this function is attributable to the existence of the depression whether of not it contains a wetland. Wetlands with a high throughflow component, such as emergent (dominated by herbaceous species) marshes in low gradient rivers, may have very little impact on flood waters.

Ground Water Recharge: Wetlands are often generically credited with the ability to supply water to underground aquifers or the shallow water table. While certain wetlands have been shown to perform this function, it is probably not widespread and is dependent on site specific conditions which are somewhat difficult to determine. Attributing this function to all wetlands is misleading. It is probably safe to say that there are more wetlands dependent on ground water as a component of their water supply than there are wetlands which effect a net recharge to an aquifer. This topic is discussed in more detail in the following section on hydrology.

Wildlife Habitat: As discussed above the fish and wildlife values of wetlands have long been recognized and served as the initial basis for wetland protection and preservation. Tidal wetlands are recognized as vital nursery grounds and foraging areas for shrimp, crabs, and other commercially valuable species of fish and shellfish. Tidal wetlands also are among the most productive ecosystems on the planet and are considered a basic component of the estuarine food web. Nontidal wetlands also provide vital habitat for many aquatic, terrestrial, and amphibious species including fish, amphibians, reptiles, waterfowl and other birds, and mammals. Nontidal wetlands encompass a vast variety of different cover types (i.e., a wide variety of herbaceous and woody plant communities) and provide critical habitat for many rare, threatened, and endangered species.

WETLAND PROCESSES

Hydrology

Hydrology is the primary factor determining the existence of wetlands; another words, without water there are no wetlands. This concept is simple, but the myriad ways in which water moves through the landscape and interacts with the physical and biotic environment makes wetland hydrology an extremely complex subject which can be difficult to study and quantify. This complexity is due in part to wetlands intermediate position between terrestrial and aquatic systems and to seasonal and longer term climatic fluctuations.

Wetland hydrology largely controls the unique biological and geochemical processes characteristic of wetlands through both the hydroperiod (or seasonal hydrology) of the wetland and the water chemistry of the incoming water. Hydrology also influences strongly influences soil type and soil processes. Lastly, wetland hydrology is the primary determinant for the vegetation community which a given wetland supports. All of these factors determine the functions and values of a given wetland. Hence, wetland hydrology has long been the basis for wetland classification systems. The critical dependence of wetlands on hydrology and their sensitivity to hydrologic change has made wetland alteration and destruction a fairly simple matter for man for thousands of years.

The manner in which water enters and leaves a wetland, which has been termed the hydrologic pathway (Mitsch and Gosselink 1986), determines the hydrology of a given wetland. Wetlands are components of the hydrologic cycle **(Figure 2.1)** and can be found across virtually the entire terrestrial portion of the cycle. Factors which influence hydrological conditions and therefore wetland occurrence are climate/precipitation, topography, geologic structure, and lithology (or rock type)**(Figure 2.2)**. The latter two factors are often combined in the term geohydrology.

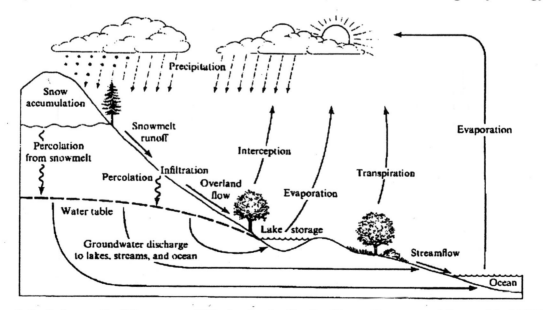

Figure 2.1. Schematic Diagram of Hydrologic Cycle (From Dunne and Leopold, 1978). Wetlands may occur throughout the terrestrial and intertidal portion of the diagram.

15

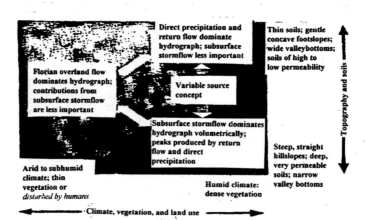

Figure 2.2. Geographic Factors Affecting Hydrology (From Dunne and Leopold, 1978).

The hydroperiod (i.e., the seasonal fluctuations of hydrology on an annual as well as a long term basis) is another important aspect of the hydrologic pathway. Hydroperiod greatly influences the rates and types of geochemical processes taking place in a wetland during the course of a year. Hydroperiod and climate are also the prime determinants controlling the type of wetland plant species present in given wetland.

Other important aspects of the hydrologic pathway which greatly influence wetland function are the quality of the incoming water in terms of water chemistry, nutrients, organic matter, pollutants, toxins, micro- and macroscopic organisms, and the rate of inflow versus outflow. This latter parameter, which controls the export rate of materials from the wetland versus the input rate, is termed throughflow or the turnover rate and is discussed in more detail below.

Evapotranspiration is another important factor affecting wetlands and wetland distribution. Evapotranspiration is the combination of evaporation, or water loss directly from surfaces back to the atmosphere, and transpiration which is water loss from plant tissues. In vegetated regions it is difficult to separate evaporation from transpiration, and the two processes are considered together under the collective term.

Wetlands derive their hydrology from precipitation, surface water, ground water, tides, or a combination thereof. Certain wetland types are characterized by an exclusive or dominant hydrology **(Figure 2.3)**:

- Tidal and mangrove wetlands are dominated by tidal hydrology;
- Bogs are typically dominated by precipitation hydrology;
- Riparian and bottomland hardwood wetlands are often dominated by river hydrology (i.e., seasonal or periodic flooding);
- Seep or spring head wetlands are dominated by ground water hydrology.

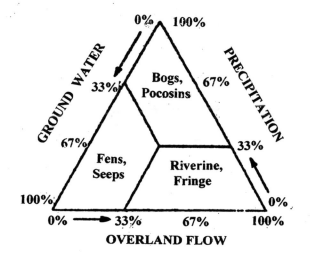

Figure 2.3. Ternary Diagram illustrating the three sources of water to wetlands and their probable relationship to several wetland types (From Brinson, 1993).

The water balance, or water budget, is a useful conceptual tool for considering the hydrology of wetlands or aquatic systems such as lakes or ponds. A water budget is the difference between inflows and outflows of water and is typically expressed as an equation (Mitsch and Gosselink 1986):

$$V^* = P + S + G - ET - S - G + T$$

where

        V = volume of water storage in wetlands

        V^* = change in volume of storage

        P = net precipitation (total prec. - interception)

        S = surface inflows (such as streams and overland flow)

        G = ground water inflows

        ET = evapotranspiration

        S = surface outflows

        G = ground water outflows

        T = tidal inflow or outflow

As one might imagine, the water budget can vary with seasonal pattern of rainfall, temperature, and growing seasons, and the relative importance of the different factors varies among wetland types and individual wetlands. Constructing a field data based water budget for a real wetland is extremely challenging because of the difficulty and expense in terms of time and money for getting accurate measurements or approximations of a number of the parameters. This is especially true for evapotranspirative losses, which can vary greatly over the course of a growing season, and in general for groundwater interactions. These variables are often estimated using mathematical models in conjunction with limited field measurements.

In considering wetland hydrology, it is important to recognize the connection between the various forms of water in the terrestrial component of the hydrologic cycle. This is particularly true for surface and shallow ground or subsurface water. In many alluvial or river valley wetlands, surface waters and shallow ground water or subsurface waters are an interconnected component of the hydrologic continuum and are difficult to separate and measure. Many wetland systems, especially in temperate regions or regions with distinct wet and dry seasons, are driven by seasonal shallow ground water or subsurface water which exists as a high water table in the early spring due to precipitation recharge over the fall and winter. This water surface gradually recedes during the growing season as evapotranspiration losses from plants exceed recharge from precipitation. In many cases this seasonal, shallow, subsurface water is hydraulically and hydrologically distinct from larger and deeper aquifers utilized for water supply throughout the year. Under certain geologic or soil conditions, shallow subsurface water can be perched on strata with low permeabilities know as aquitards. This can also create seasonal ponding which supports wetlands. Vernal pools are one type of wetland characterized by this type of hydrology, though not all vernal pools require the presence of perched water tables or aquitards.

Another useful wetland hydrology concept, related to the overall hydrologic budget, which greatly influences the function of a given wetland is the degree of openness or through flow. This concept is termed the turnover rate in studies of lakes and ponds. It is a measure of the replacement rate of the water volume within the system. The time required for a complete replacement or turnover of the water is termed the residence time. The openness or throughflow rate influences not only the delivery of water (and whatever the water is carrying in terms of water chemistry and other material to the wetland), but the export of water and other substances from the wetland.

Biogeochemical Processes

Biogeochemical processes are an essential component of all ecosystems. These processes, in conjunction with hydrological processes, cycle and recycle materials and compounds within and between ecosystems. Materials may be imported, exported, stored temporarily or permanently, and/or transformed into different states or compounds. An example of a major biogeochemical process would be the breakdown of organic carbon by fungi and bacteria as garden composting. In this process complex organic carbon chains, which cannot be absorbed by plants, are broken down or transformed into a series of less complex constituents. One by-product is ammonium, a form of nitrogen which is an important nutrient for plants. Once in this form, the compound can be absorbed by plants and converted once more to complex carbon chains through photosynthesis. In terrestrial systems, bacteria, fungi, and other microbes, algae, and plants residing in or on the surface of the soil are key agents in biogeochemical cycling and dominate transformation processes.

Biogeochemical processes in wetlands are unique because of the hydrologic conditions which create saturated soils for all or part of the year. When a soil is saturated, water occupies the voids or interstitial pore spaces, and greatly reduces oxygen diffusion into and within the soil. Any oxygen present is rapidly depleted by aerobic microbial respiration. In an upland soil, the voids would typically contain atmospheric gases, the most important of which for dictating microbial processes is oxygen. When oxygen is present, the system is dominated by aerobic microbes and oxidation processes. Under saturated conditions oxygen is limited or absent, and the system is dominated by anaerobic microbes and reduction processes.

The effects of oxidation versus reduction are illustrated by the transformations of the element iron (Fe). Iron in upland, mineral soils generally occurs in an oxidized or ferric state (Fe+++, as in Fe(OH)3) with its characteristic brown or reddish color. It is ferric iron in conjunction with oxidized manganese that gives many upland soils the brown to red/orange tint. In a wetland reducing environment, iron occurs in a reduced or ferrous state (Fe++, as in Fe(OH)2) and has a characteristic gray/green color. Reduced iron in combination with reduced manganese and sulfur combine to create a very dark grey to blue/black soil color in saturated, wetland, mineral soils. This soil coloring process due to reduction is termed gleying, and soils exhibiting these effects are described as gleyed. When gleying occurs at or near the surface, it is diagnostic of wetland conditions. In general, the more saturated the soils, the more intense the gleying and the darker the coloration.

In seasonally saturated wetland mineral soils, the soil column typically exhibits a gray matrix with interspersed reddish mottles. When found at or near the surface, this coloration is also a diagnostic feature of wetland mineral soils; the gray matrix results from the prevailing saturated conditions (reduced iron and manganese giving the color), and the red or orange mottles results from oxygen diffusion into the soil column during the dry season when the water table is lower. These color features are not present in all wetland soils. Organic (peaty) and sandy wetland soils do not exhibit these diagnostic color features.

The gleyed and mottled mineral soil color features are indicative of the range of reducing environments in wetlands and the type of chemical transformations which can occur in such environments. What are perhaps more important in terms of beneficial wetland functions are other associated anaerobic processes and their effects on other elements and compounds such as the nutrients (nitrogen and phosphorous) and carbon.

The major nutrients, nitrogen and phosphorous, are essential for plant growth, and control productivity in ecosystems, and their cycling within ecosystems is controlled by biogeochemical processes. Additions of nutrients can often increase productivity in ecosystems, but when oversupplied, nutrients become pollutants with severe, deleterious effects on ecosystems. This is particularly well documented in aquatic ecosystems where accelerated nutrient enrichment of ponds, lakes, and estuaries, often termed eutrophication, can have degradational effects. Oversupply of nutrients can cause population explosions of algae and other phytoplankton which, as they decompose, can deplete dissolved oxygen in the water body leading to stress and/or death for fish and other aerobic organisms.

The biogeochemical pathways of nitrogen in the environment are complex and are described as the nitrogen cycle. This is a natural recycling system which cycles nitrogen between the atmosphere, the earth, and organisms through multiple pathways. Wetlands play a key role in the nitrogen cycle. Denitrification, in which nitrogen in nitrate form (NO_3-) is converted to nitrogen gas (N_2) and returned to the atmosphere is perhaps one of the more important of the wetland transformation processes affecting water quality. In this process, anaerobic bacteria utilizing organic carbon as a substrate and energy source, convert nitrate nitrogen to nitrogen gas. A number of studies have documented that wetlands can intercept nitrogen (nitrate) laden runoff from agricultural fields, retain it, and convert much of the nitrate to nitrogen gas (N2). Under ideal conditions, the nitrogen concentration in the water subsequently leaving the wetland may have be reduced by as much as 90% (Corell and Peterjohn 1984). The denitrification process is significant in many but not all wetlands. The process is inhibited by low pH and peat and is of lesser import in northern peatlands and acid bogs.

Nitrogen in ammonium (NH4+) form can also be immobilized through attachment to soil particles. Because of these and other chemical transformations, nitrogen is often the limiting nutrient for plant growth in wetlands.

Wetlands have also been shown to remove phosphorous from the water, but the phosphorous removal is primarily due to the physical deposition and retention of very fine sediment particles (clay particles) to which phosphorous attaches or adsorbs. This wetland water quality effect may be most pronounced in bottomland and floodplain wetlands during seasonal, overbank flood events as current velocities decrease, and the fine sediment particles settle out of the water column. However, in some cases wetlands have been shown to be net exporters of phosphorous (Mitsch and Gosselink 1984). The anaerobic conditions which aid the denitrification process may actually transform insoluble forms of phosphorous into soluble forms which can then flow out of the wetland.

This brings us to the complex topic of whether wetlands function as sinks or sources of nutrients and other compounds. Some wetlands have been shown to function as sinks for particular compounds and sources for others. Studies have documented both effects and suggest that net effects can vary seasonally or year to year in a given wetland as well as among different wetland types. However, it is generally accepted that many wetlands are sinks for certain inorganic nutrients and sources of organic compounds. The role of an individual wetland in these sink/source functions is dependent on many factors including hydrology, chemical input, and position in the landscape.

On a global scale, the sink/source role of wetlands has become an important question regarding global warming and the greenhouse effect. The bogs of northern North America and Eurasia may account for as much as 56% of global methane production (Matthew and Fung 1987). While methane is not as abundant a carbon dioxide, the primary greenhouse gas, methane is twenty times more efficient at trapping heat than carbon dioxide. While there is no consensus of opinion on the this topic, many scientists believe that global warming could lead to increased methane production as the northern wetlands warm, initiating a positive feedback process which could dramatically accelerate global warming.

Plant Adaptations for Life in Wetlands

The saturated conditions of wetlands which affect biogeochemical conditions in wetland soils also profoundly influence plants. Wetland or hydrophytic plants have evolved a range of adaptations to cope with wetland conditions. These adaptations or hydrophytic characteristics are most pronounced in species occupying continuously saturated soils which are termed "obligate" wetland plants (see Chapter 3). Hydrophytic characteristics are less pronounced in species which occupy seasonally saturated wetlands, and upland plants cannot survive in soils saturated for more than several weeks.

The primary factor affecting plants in wetland environments is the absence or low level of soil oxygen. Plant roots require oxygen for vital metabolic processes, and without oxygen suffer root anoxia. Wetland species have evolved specialized cell structures which permit diffusion of oxygen from the aerial portions of the plant down into the roots. These "aerenchymous" tissues are most pronounced in obligate wetland species. The biogeochemical transformations in wetland soils also effect other aspects of plant biology from nutrient uptake to reproduction. In addition wetlands are subjected to regular or irregular periods of drying. Salts in marine and estuarine tidal waters are an additional stress which has required elaborate adaptations. These combined effects require both physiological and ecological adaptations for plant and animal life (Mitsch and Gosselink 1986). For a more detailed discussion the reader is referred to the cited reference.

Landscape Perspective

Wetland scientists have increasingly recognized that the factors controlling the existence of a wetland as well as its functions and values are largely determined by landscape characteristics and the wetland's position in the landscape. Position in the landscape can be defined as topographic or spatial location relative to the drainage network of streams and rivers, other wetlands, topography, and other landscape features such as forests or agricultural fields. Landscape position in many cases determines wetland hydrology, throughflow, and the delivery and type of materials coming into a wetland. These physical factors dictate wetland function and ultimately wetland value.

The landscape perspective provides for the evaluation of wetland impacts in the context of the larger system in which the wetland functions. This systems approach to wetland function is gradually being incorporated in regulatory and management policy where it is sometimes termed "cumulative impact analysis". While this approach is an intuitively logical one for systems ecologists, hydrologists, and geomorphologists, our knowledge of wetland functions and landscape processes is often insufficient for the definitive determination of the relative value of individual wetlands within a system. However, there is general agreement that this is the direction in which to proceed to better manage and regulate or wetland resources.

The new Hydrogeomorphic Wetland Classification System (Brinson 1993) is a functional assessment based classification system incorporating the landscape approach. The hydrogeomorphic approach has been developed over the last several years to serve as the basis for the U.S. Army Corps of Engineers functional assessment model which is in development. The goal of the program is to develop a function based assessment model which can yield effective information across the range of wetland types and geographic conditions found in the United States. The Hydrogeomorphic Classification system is discussed in more detail in the next chapter.

CHAPTER THREE
WETLAND CLASSIFICATION

Published wetland classification systems date back to the beginning of this century. Not surprisingly, the earlier efforts focussed on northern peatlands and bogs since this is the dominant wetland type in much of Europe. Most wetland classification systems are based on hydrology which is the dominant factor controlling wetland location and type.

The first comprehensive effort in the U.S. which attempted to deal with all wetland types was the 1956 U.S. Fish and Wildlife Service publication mentioned above, Circular 39. The actual title for this work is *Wetlands of the United States, Their Extent, and Their Value for Waterfowl and Other Wildlife* which reflects the previously mentioned appreciation of wetlands in this country almost solely as waterfowl habitat. This classification system was developed in conjunction with a national inventory of wetlands. This descriptive system divided all wetlands into four types: inland freshwater, inland saline, coastal freshwater, and coastal saline. The second hierarchy was based on hydroperiod (if seasonally inundated) or depth (if permanently inundated).

Circular 39 was the dominant wetland classification system until 1979 when the U.S. Fish and Wildlife Service published the *Classification of Wetlands and Deepwater Habitats of the United States*. This classification scheme, which is referred to as the Cowardin System after the lead author, is the predominant classification system used in the U.S. today. It includes what are typically thought of as aquatic ecosystems (i.e., "deepwater" habitats) because they are so often proximal to "real" wetlands. Again, this reflects the difficulty in defining where wetlands begin and end on the aquatic as well as upland boundary.

The Cowardin approach is an hierarchical classification which is based on five major hydrologic regimes or systems: marine, estuarine, palustrine, lacustrine, or riverine. These major hierarchies are in turn subdivided into subsystems, classes, subclasses, and modifiers and submodifiers **(Figure 3.1)**. The subsystems further modify the hydrologic regime while the classes describe the habitat type (rock bottom to forest in the Palustrine system). This system was also devised for inventory purposes serving as the basis for the photointerpretive mapping of wetlands for the U.S. Fish and Wildlife Service's National Wetland Inventory. These maps, which are available for much of the U.S. on the quadrangle system used for the U.S. Geological Survey quadrangle maps, generally serve as excellent guidelines for assessing wetland resources on a broad scale. However, they are not sufficient for determining the extent of wetland resources on a site nor for delineation or determination of acreage of potential impacts.

Several recent approaches to wetland classification are worthy of note. The U.S. Army Corps of Engineers, Environmental Laboratory developed a hydrologic based classification system for nontidal wetlands as a component of the *1987 Corps of Engineers Wetland Delineation Manual*. This system divides nontidal wetlands into five different hydrologic regimes: (1) permanently inundated, (2) semipermanently to nearly permanently inundated, (3) regularly inundated or saturated, (4) seasonally inundated or saturated, and (5) irregularly inundated or saturated. This system is essentially an enhancement of the Circular 39 classification system for inland freshwater wetlands but does not incorporate a dominant vegetative community descriptor. It is a pure hydrologic regime system, and can provide a first step for the functional description of a wetland for delineation or assessment purposes.

The most recent classification system is the Hydrogeomorphic Wetland Classification (HGM) System (Brinson 1993). This system has been developed as the foundation for the U.S. Army Corps of Engineers's effort to develop a wetland functional assessment model. The HGM approach is based on the assumption that physical factors are the prime determinants of wetland function and that biotic community type is likewise dependent on the same physical factors (i.e., wetland plant

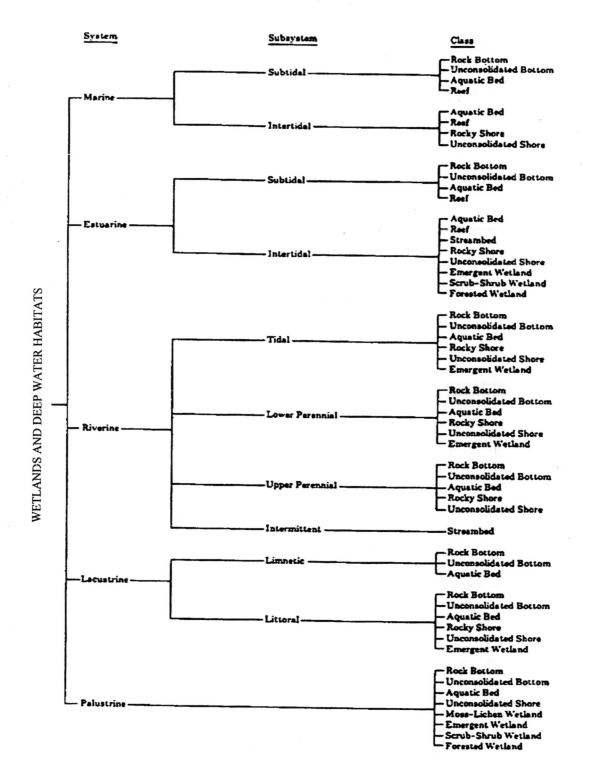

Figure 3.1. Wetland and Deepwater Classification System, Systems, and Classes (From Cowardin, et al, 1979).

community cover type). The three parameters on which this system is based are: (1) hydrodynamics, (2) water source and water transport, and (3) geomorphic setting or the wetland's position in the landscape. There are broad subdescriptors for each of these three parameters. It is recognized in that the three parameters are inherently interrelated: geomorphic setting often determines hydrodynamics and water source and water transport; water source will often determine hydrodynamics. The system also recognizes that a given wetland may exhibit more than one type of water source. A wetland in a floodplain may be both a depressional wetland supplied by shallow groundwater and runoff as well as a riverine wetland which is seasonally or episodically inundated by flooding. The interrelatedness in this functional based classification system reflects the various environmental gradients which control wetland occurrence and wetland type.

Despite the name, the HGM's geomorphic component is very limited, and the system would be much more valuable if this element were expanded. This expansion would be most feasible and useful if conducted at the regional level (e.g., the eco-region level) where a landscape level geomorphic factor would provide a detailed context for wetland function and value assessment, whereas the HGM attempts to encompass the entire country. As it stands now this classification is simply an enhanced hydrology based system.

But the hydrogeomorphic system does provide an initial basis for a landscape level, functional assessment for wetland management and decision making. It is relatively simple to apply in the field and can provide a valuable perspective on the functional values of an individual wetland as well as on multiple wetlands within a drainage basin or landscape. However, since its focus is on the dominant physical factors affecting function it does not include a cover type modifier or vegetative community descriptor. Therefore the HGM is most useful when used in conjunction with another system which addresses the vegetative or biotic component. The Cowardin System is the most sophisticated descriptive system. It was designed for and is best suited for large scale mapping or analyzing wetland trends (i.e., losses) on a regional or larger scale. It also has the advantage of being the dominant descriptive system utilized by wetland scientists and regulators and provides an immediate reference base for discussion. However, it does not include a functional component (Krause 1994).

The HGM in combination with the Cowardin System can provide a thorough description of a wetland or wetland system. This combined approach would allow experienced wetland scientists and regulators to analyze potential impacts, assess cumulative impacts, assess the alternatives analysis and avoidance and minimization measures, and evaluate any proposed mitigation measures during the design and engineering of projects which involve potential wetland impacts. This after all is the purpose of the 404 program as it is currently applied.

CHAPTER FOUR
WETLAND DELINEATION

In Chapter 2 we described the position of wetlands in the landscape as transitional or intermediate between upland and aquatic systems and briefly discussed the potential difficulty of determining the precise endpoint of a wetland. While some wetlands may end abruptly and therefore be readily delineated in the field, in many cases the wetland/upland or wetland/open water interface is a gradational zone, a part of the landscape continuum from water to upland. In this zone wetland characteristics decrease as upland or open water characteristics increase, subject to subtle seasonal shifts or more pronounced oscillations over decades or centuries due to climatic fluctuations. Determination of an exact and legally defensible wetland boundary in the field is the challenge of wetland delineation. And, as also mentioned in Chapter 2, such a determination is impossible without a wetland definition based on detailed, discernable field parameters, and, perhaps more importantly, a prescribed methodology for determining wetland boundaries in the field. The current methodology for the field determination of a wetland is the *1987 Corps of Engineers Wetland Delineation Manual* (the "1987 Manual" or "Corps Manual"). This chapter will provide an overview of the methodology specified in this document. The reader should refer to the 1987 Manual and the U.S. Army Corps of Engineers's many Regulatory Guidance Letters for more detailed information and discussion.

But first a little recent history of delineation methodologies. The 1987 Manual was replaced in January 1989 by the *1989 Federal Manual for Identifying and Delineation Jurisdictional Wetlands* (the "1989 Manual"). The 1989 Manual had been developed jointly by the U.S. Army Corps of Engineers (the Corps), the Environmental Protection Agency (EPA), the U.S. Department of Agriculture Soil Conservation Service (SCS), and the U.S. Fish and Wildlife Service (USFWS). All of these agencies had been involved to greater or lesser extent in the management, identification, and or delineation of wetlands under various federal laws, and several of the agencies had independently developed technical criteria, field indicators, and or methodology for wetlands identification and boundary determination. Then, in August 1991, use of the 1989 Manual was suspended. The 1989 Manual's suspension was based on various "concerns" identified by the Corps, the EPA, the Soil Conservation Service, and the USFWS and public comments. Some of the concerns were: that wetlands determinations based on less than all three of the basic parameters (vegetation, soils, and hydrology) and sometimes one, that seven days of water was not sufficient to create a wetland, that areas with a dry surface but water present as deep as 18 inches below ground could be considered wetlands, and that the 1989 Manual was developed without meaningful public support. The 1987 Manual was reinstated for all new delineations (all delineations completed under the 1989 Manual were grandfathered though the land owner had the option to re-delineate under the 1987 Manual and use which ever was more favorable), and the National Research Council of National Academy of Sciences was charged by Congress with reviewing the existing federal definition of a wetland its application for the identification and delineation of wetlands. The Committee on Wetlands Characterization, which was appointed in July 1993, was planning to release their report in early 1995. The report may lead to changes in the federal definition and delineation procedures, but until any changes are authorized by congress, the 1987 Manual is still the law of the land for wetland identification and delineation.

The 1987 Manual provides methodologies for:

1. Identifying or determining an area as a wetland subject to federal jurisdiction; and

2. Determining the boundary of the wetland.

The 1987 Manual was designed to identify and delineate wetlands on the basis of the three parameters in the current definition of wetlands: vegetation, soils, and hydrology. For field identification and delineation these three parameters must be defined in much greater detail than in the one-paragraph federal definition, and in terms which can be measured, observed, or inferred in the field. Over one quarter of the 98-page text of the 1987 Manual is devoted to "Technical Guidelines" for the identification and delineation of wetlands and "Characteristics and indicators of Hydrophytic Vegetation, Hydric Soils, and Wetland Hydrology".

The technical guidelines **(Table 4.1)** provide straight-forward, diagnostic definitions of the environmental characteristics of wetlands, deepwater aquatic habitats, and nonwetlands on the basis of the three parameter approach. These guidelines provide the methodology for determining if an area is a wetland versus an aquatic habitat or upland, the first step in the determination of an area as a wetland or not.

The three parameters are further defined and discussed "Characteristics and Indicators of Hydrophytic Vegetation, Hydric Soils, and Wetland Hydrology". This section provides the essential, detailed information for the analysis of the three parameters in the field as well as conceptual support for the working definition of wetlands in the 1987 Manual. The characteristics are given first followed by the rules for indicator determination. A summary of the characteristics and indicator section follows.

Table 4.1. **Technical Guidelines for the identification of wetlands versus deepwater aquatic habitats and non wetlands** (From the 1987 *Corps of Engineers Wetland Delineation Manual*, pages 13-15).

Wetlands

a.   Definition - The Corps of Engineers (*Federal Register* 1982) and the EPA (*Federal Register* 1980) jointly define wetlands as: those areas that are inundated or saturated by surface or ground water at a frequency and duration sufficient to support, and that under normal circumstances do support, a prevalence of vegetation typically adapted for life in saturated soil conditions. Wetlands generally include swamps, marshes, bogs, and similar areas.

b.   Diagnostic, general, environmental characteristics of wetlands:

   1.   Vegetation - the prevalent vegetation consists of macrophytes that are typically adapted to areas having hydrologic and soil conditions as described above. Hydrophytic species, due to morphological, physiological, and/or reproductive adaptation(s), have the ability to grow, effectively compete, reproduce, and/or persist in anaerobic soil conditions.

   2.   Soil - soils are present and have been classified as hydric, or they possess characteristics that are associated with reducing soil conditions.

   3.   Hydrology - the area is inundated either permanently or periodically at mean water depths 6.6 feet or less, or the soil is saturated to the surface at some time during the growing season of the prevalent vegetation.

c.   Technical approach for the identification and delineation of wetlands - Except in certain situations defined in this manual, evidence of a minimum of one positive wetland indicator from each parameter (hydrology, soil, and vegetation) must be found in order to make a positive wetland determination.

Deepwater Aquatic Habitats

a.   Definition - Deepwater aquatic habitats area areas that are permanently inundated at mean annual water depths greater than 6.6 feet or permanently inundated areas less than or equal to 6.6 feet in depth that do not support rooted emergent of woody plant species.[1]

b.   Diagnostic environmental characteristics:

   1.   Vegetation - no rooted emergent or woody plant species are present in these permanently inundated areas.

---

[1] Areas less than or equal to 6.6 feet in mean annual depth that support only submergent aquatic plants (seaweeds, pondweeds, etc.) are vegetated shallows, not wetlands

Table 4.1 (continued)

2.   Soil - the substrate technically is not defined as a soil if the mean water depth is greater than 6.6 feet or if it will not support rooted emergent or woody plants.

     3.   Hydrology - the area is permanently inundated at mean water depths greater than 6.6 feet.

c.   Technical approach for the identification and delineation of deepwater aquatic habitats - When any one of the diagnostic characteristics identified above is present, the area is a deepwater habitat.

Nonwetlands

a.   Definition - Nonwetlands include uplands and lowland areas that are neither deepwater aquatic habitat, wetlands, nor other aquatic sites. They are seldom or never inundated, or if frequently inundated, they have saturated soils for only brief periods during the growing season, and, if vegetated, they normally support a prevalence of vegetation typically adapted for life only in aerobic soil conditions.[2]

b.   Diagnostic environmental characteristics:

     1.   Vegetation - the prevalent vegetation consists of plant species that are typically adapted for life only in aerobic soils. These mesophytic and/or xerophytic macrophytes cannot persist in predominantly anaerobic soil conditions.

     2.   Soil - Soils, when present, are not classified as hydric, and possess characteristics associated with aerobic conditions.

     3.   Hydrology - although the soil may be inundated or saturated by surface water or ground water periodically during the growing season of the prevalent vegetation, the average annual duration of inundation or soil saturation does not preclude the occurrence of plant species typically adapted for life in aerobic conditions.

c.   Technical approach for the identification and delineation of nonwetlands - When any one of the diagnostic characteristics identified above is present, the area is a nonwetland.

---

     [2] Some species, due to their broad ecological tolerances, occur in both wetlands and nonwetlands (e.g., Red maple (*Acer rubrum*).

HYDROPHYTIC VEGETATION

Characteristics

Hydrophytic vegetation is defined as:

the sum total of macrophytic plant life that occurs in areas where the frequency and duration of inundation or soil saturation produce permanently or periodically saturated soils of sufficient duration to exert a controlling influence on the plant species present.

Hydrophytic vegetation for the purposes of the 1987 Manual is also defined as macroscopic vegetation as opposed to microscopic vegetation. The authors of the 1987 Manual elected to adopt the "plant community" and "prevalence" approach versus an indicator species approach. This is a concept basic to plant ecology which recognizes that plants rarely occur in monotypic stands in nature but rather in mixed groupings or associations of several to many species. Plant communities or associations therefore are best described on the basis of the dominant or prevalent species. Numerous sampling techniques have been developed to determine dominant species. Difficulties arise because of the diversity of plant community types and the necessity of different dominance determination methodologies for woody and herbaceous plant communities. What this means is that the presence of several typically upland species in an area dominated by hydrophytic vegetation would not preclude the area from being considered a wetland. Nor would the presence of several hydrophytic species confirm an area as a wetland.

The next key word in the definition, "typically adapted", is also clarified. Wetlands are characterized by soils saturated for at least part of the year which creates anaerobic conditions. Wetland plants exhibit physiological adaptations for anaerobic conditions. If the dominant plants exhibit such adaptations, then the hydrophytic vegetation test is met. However, since there are virtually infinite degrees of wetness in the wetland universe, there are is vast assemblage of plant species which may in and across the boundaries of wetland types. Some species are wetland endemics, occurring almost always in wetland environments. And there are many species with a broad "ecological amplitude" which may occur in wetlands or uplands.

In order to reduce potential confusion, the Plant Indicator Status Categories were developed and applied to each species listed in the National List of Plant Species that Occur in Wetlands which includes over 5,000 plants. The five categories and their respective, estimated probability of occurrence are presented in **Table 4.2**. The categories range from "obligate" wetland species, those which occur in wetlands 99% of the time, to obligate upland species, those which occur in uplands 99% of the time. The middle category, facultative, includes plants with a broad ecological amplitude. These plants have an even chance of occurring in wetland or uplands.

Table 4.2. **Plant Indicator Status Categories** (From the 1987 *Corps of Engineers Wetland Delineation Manual*, page 18).

Indicator Category	Indicator Symbol	Definition
OBLIGATE WETLAND PLANTS	OBL	Plants that occur almost always (estimated probability >99%) in wetlands under natural conditions, but which may also occur rarely (estimated probability <1%) in nonwetlands. Examples: Salt marsh cordgrass (*Spartina alterniflora*), Bald cypress (*Taxodium distichum*)
FACULTATIVE WETLAND PLANTS	FACW	Plants that occur usually (estimated probability >67% to 99%) in wetlands, but also occur (estimated probability 1% to 33% in nonwetlands). Examples: Green ash (*Fraxinus pennsylvanica*), Red osier dogwood (*Cornus stolonifera*).

Table 4.2 (continued)		
FACULTATIVE PLANTS	FAC	Plants with a similar likelihood (estimated probability 33% to 67%) of occurring in both wetlands and nonwetlands. Examples: Honey locust (*Gleditsia tricanthos*), Greenbriar (*Smilax rotundifolia*).
FACULTATIVE UPLAND PLANTS	FACU	Plants that occur sometimes (estimated probability 1% to <33%) in wetlands, but occur more often (estimated probability >67% to 99%) in nonwetlands. Examples: Northern red oak (*Quercus rubra*), Tall cinquefoil (*Potentilla arguta*).
OBLIGATE UPLAND PLANTS	UPL	Plants that rarely (estimated probability <1%) in wetlands, but occur almost always (estimated probability >99%) in nonwetlands under natural conditions. Examples: Short leaf pine (*Pinus echinata*), Soft chess (*Bromus mollis*).

The categories and plant list were originally developed by the U.S. Fish and Wildlife Service for the National Wetlands Inventory. The list has been modified and is periodically reviewed by the National Plant List Panel. A series of regional plant lists, subsets of the national list, has also been published by the Corps of Engineers (**Table 4.3**). The intent of these lists is to provide more accurate indicator status for a given species in region than is possible at the national level. The indicator status listings can be further supplemented by the Fish and Wildlife Service's ecological profiles of regional, wetland community types.

Table 4.3.	List of Corps of Engineers' Preliminary Wetland Guides (From the 1987 Corps of Engineers Wetland Delineation Manual, page 20).		
Region		Publication Date	WES* Report No.
Peninsular Florida		Feb. 1978	TR Y-78-2
Puerto Rico		April 1978	TR Y-78-3
West Coast States		April 1978	TR Y-78-4
Gulf Coastal Plain		May 1978	TR Y-78-5
Interior		May 1982	TR Y-78-6
South Atlantic States		May 1982	TR Y-78-7
North Atlantic States		May 1982	TR Y-78-8
Alaska		Feb. 1984	TR Y-78-9

* Waterway Experiment Station

Indicators of Hydrophytic Vegetation

The indicators for hydrophytic vegetation are presented in hierarchical order of "reliability" in the 1987 Manual as listed below:

1. Fifty percent or more of the *dominant* species have an obligate (OBL), facultative wet (FACWET), or facultative (FAC) indicator status. (Methodologies for dominance determination are presented in the next section of field methods.)

2. Presence of plant species which, based on the delineator's knowledge and experience, typically grow in areas of prolonged inundation and/or saturated soils.

41

3.   Morphological adaptations for survival in areas of prolonged inundation and/or saturated soils. (A number of wetland plants exhibit macroscopic, morphological features developed for survival in wetland conditions; examples include "buttressed" trunks and shallow root systems. These features are discussed in detail in the appendices to the 1987 Manual.).

4.   Documentation of a species typical occurrence in wetlands in the technical literature.

The 1987 Manual clearly states that in the vast majority of cases only the first indicator should be used. The other three indicators are to be used as supporting evidence only. If one of the last three is the basis for the determination, then the decision should be second guessed prior to finalizing the determination. The last three indicators, with the possible exception of item 2, are essentially redundant since they are already incorporated in the national and regional listings of plant species likely to occur in wetlands. Item 2 recognizes that experienced wetland scientists and delineators may be aware of species which in a region or sub-region typically occur in wetland environments yet are not listed or incorrectly listed in the national or regional lists of plants typically occurring in wetlands.

HYDRIC SOILS

Characteristics

A hydric soil is defined as "a soil that is saturated, flooded, or ponded long enough during the growing season to develop anaerobic conditions that favor the growth and regeneration of hydrophytic vegetation" (U.S. Dept. of Agriculture Soil

Conservation Service 1985, as amended by the National Technical Committee for Hydric Soils in December 1986). The National Technical Committee developed the following criteria for hydric soils using the Soil Conservation Service's soil nomenclature:

A.   All histosols (organic soils such as peat) except folists;

B.   Soils in Aquic suborders, Aquic subgroups, Albols suborder, Salorthids great group, or Pell great groups of Vertisols that are:

   1.   Somewhat poorly drained and have a water table less than 0.5 feet from the surface for a significant period (usually a week or more) during the growing season, or

   2.   Poorly drained or very poorly drained and have either:

      a.   a water table at less than 1.0 feet from the surface for a significant period (usually a week or more) during the growing season if permeability is equal to or greater than 6.0 inches/hour in all layers within 20 inches; or

      b.   a water table at less than 1.5 feet from the surface for a significant period (usually a week or more) during the growing season; or

C.   Soils that are ponded for a long or very long duration during the growing season; or

D.   Soils that are frequently flooded for long duration or very long duration during the growing season.

Drained soils are discussed in some detail. Drainage may result in a situation where the soil is technically a hydric soils but no longer has the hydrology to support hydrophytic plants; hence all areas with hydric soils are not necessarily wetlands. General background information on soils including a definition of soils, soil horizon descriptions, factors influencing soils and hydric soils in particular, and a very brief discussion of soil classification are also provided.

Hydric Soil Indicators

This section is divided into nonsandy soils and sandy soils because of the very different nature of hydric characteristics in sandy soils. The indicators are listed in order of decreasing reliability, and confirmation of any one characteristic is indicative of a hydric soil. We have listed only the indicator characteristics below; for additional explanation and discussion please refer to the 1987 Manual.

Nonsandy Soil Indicators
A.   Organic soils (Histosols)

B.   Histic epipedons

C.   Sulfidic material

D.   Aquic or peraquic moisture regime

E.   Reducing soil conditions

F.   Soil colors

1. gleyed soils (gray colors)

2. soils with bright mottles and/or low matrix chroma

G.   Soils appearing on the hydric soil lists (based on the National List of Hydric Soils prepared by the National Technical Committee on

Hydric Soils which is included in an appendix in the manual; hydric soil lists are also available for many states which may include soils not listed on the national list)

H.   Iron and manganese concretions

Sandy Soil Indicators

A.   High organic matter content in surface horizon

B.   Streaking of subsurface horizons by organic matter

C.   Organic pans

WETLAND HYDROLOGY

Characteristics

The term "wetland hydrology" is defined as encompassing "all hydrologic characteristics of areas that are periodically inundated or have soils saturated to the surface at some time during the growing season". The 1987 Manual describes hydrology as "the least exact of the parameters", and emphasizes the potential difficulty of confirming hydrology in the field. Hydrology is easily confirmed on at least a daily basis in tidal wetlands, but in many nontidal wetlands hydrology is visually evident only on a seasonal basis (e.g., spring high water table or floods) or sporadic basis (e.g., precipitation and/or runoff). If the delineator visits such a site during a dryer period it may be difficult to document hydrology.

A discussion of factors potentially influencing wetland hydrology is followed by a discussion of classification efforts. A classification system for the hydrology of nontidal wetlands is presented in **Table 4.4.**

Table 4.4. **Hydrologic Classification System for Nontidal Areas (From the 1987** *Corps of Engineers Wetland Delineation Manual*, page 36).

Zone	Zone	Duration	Comments
I	Permanently inundated	100%	Inundation >6.6 ft. mean water depth
II	Semipermanently to nearly permanently inundated or saturated	>75% – >100%	Inundation defined as ≤6.6 ft. water depth
III	Regularly inundated or saturated	>25% – 75%	
IV	Seasonally inundated or saturated	>12.5% – 25%	
V	Irregularly inundated or saturated	≥5% – 12.5%	Many areas having these hydrologic characteristics are not wetlands
VI	Intermittently or never inundated or saturated	<5%	Areas with these hydrologic characteristics are not wetlands

Indicators of Wetland Hydrology

Indicators of wetland hydrology are numerous and are somewhat dependent on geographic location and climate (desert versus boreal environments) and position in the landscape (floodplain versus hill slope). The following list of indicators, presented in the 1987 Manual, is divided into recorded data and field (observational) data:

A.   Recorded Data - Stream gage data, lake gage data, tidal gage data, flood predictions, and historical data may be available from the following sources:

1.   Corps of Engineers District Offices
2.   U.S. Geological Survey (USGS)
3.   State, county, and local agencies
4.   Soil Conservation Service Small Watershed Projects
5.   Planning documents of developers

B.   Field Data - The following field hydrologic indicators can be assessed quickly, and although some of them are not necessarily indicative of hydrologic events that occur only during the growing season, they do provide evidence that inundation and/or soil saturation has occurred:

1.   Visual observation of inundation
2.   Visual observation of soil saturation
3.   Watermarks
4.   Driftlines
5.   Sediment deposits
6.   Drainage patterns within wetlands

FIELD METHODS

Part IV of the 1987 Manual describes the methodology(ies) for conducting wetland delineations in the field. There are five basic components: preliminary data gathering procedures, "routine determination" procedures, "comprehensive determination" procedures, "atypical situation" determination procedures, and "problem areas". All wetland delineations use either routine or comprehensive approach initially, and are based on the positive or negative indicators of the three parameters. If one of the three parameters is absent due to recent alteration, then the atypical situation method is used to determine the status of the parameter. If one of the three parameters is absent due to "normal" seasonal or annual fluctuations, then the problem area method is applied for that parameter(s). Neither the atypical situation nor the problem area methods are intended to extend jurisdiction over areas that do not exhibit positive indicators of the three parameters.

The routine method is the most frequently used. It is a "qualitative" method in that the delineator investigates the three parameters to determine if wetlands are present, and, if the answer is yes, then locates the wetland boundary on the basis of the of the three parameter's in the field. The comprehensive method involves a more elaborate, and labor intensive sampling approach where the vegetative parameter is quantitatively analyzed with sampling plots. This method is typically used in the larger and more complex or difficult field situations and/or when "rigid" documentation is required. The atypical situation procedure is used only when the routine or comprehensive methods have been applied, and it has been determined that positive indicators of one or more of the three parameters had been obliterated due to recent human disturbance or natural events. The problem areas category exists for those *natural* wetland types and/or conditions where positive indication of one or more of the three parameters may be difficult or impossible for at least some period of the year. The five components are discussed in a little more detail below. For more extensive discussion see the 1987 Manual.

Preliminary Data Gathering

The preliminary data gathering section details sources for the type of information useful for making a wetland determination. This information is not necessarily required for making a determination, but analysis of such information will facilitate the determination and potentially save time and effort. Of course the level of information available will vary somewhat for different sites and regions of the country. The following typical information sources are listed and described in the 1987 Manual:

- U.S. Geological Survey (USGS) topographic quadrangle maps
- National Wetland Inventory (NWI) maps
- National List of Plants that Occur in Wetlands (Appendix C in 1987 Manual)
- U.S. Department of Agriculture county Soil Surveys
- Stream and tidal gage data (USGS)
- Aerial photographs and remote sensing data illustrating land cover
- State, county, and local government information such as topographic maps, etc.
- other studies which may include wetland delineations on adjacent properties, environmental impact studies, etc.
- local individuals and experts
- applicant's survey plans and engineering designs

The most useful information for most applications are the soil surveys, recent aerial photographs, and topographic maps at scales of 1" = 200' or better.

The 1987 Manual goes on to list a detailed series of steps to follow for the analysis and synthesis of the information gathered prior to initiation of the field effort. This information is used at least initially, for the selection of the appropriate method to make the determination.

Routine Determinations

As described above the routine determination is the most frequently used method. The routine method is divided into three levels:

Level 1 - onsite inspection unnecessary
Level 2 - onsite inspection necessary

Level 3 - combination of Levels 1 and 2

Detailed procedures for the application of all three levels are presented in the 1987 Manual including the equipment required. Flow charts illustrating the steps in Levels 1 and 2 are given in **Figures 4.1** and **4.2,** respectively. Level 2 is the most commonly applied method in nontidal wetland delineations. Level 2 is applied slightly differently for small sites and large sites. For sites less than or equal to five acres, the determination and delineation is conducted somewhat randomly through traverses of the site. For sites larger than five acres a baseline parallel to the long axis of the site is set up with transects across the site perpendicular to the baseline. The delineator walks the transects to analyze the three parameters and make the wetland determination and delineation. However, this latter approach may not be practical on many large sites with nontidal wetlands occurring along or adjacent to small streams or creeks. The wetland delineator must often adapt the methodology to the site.

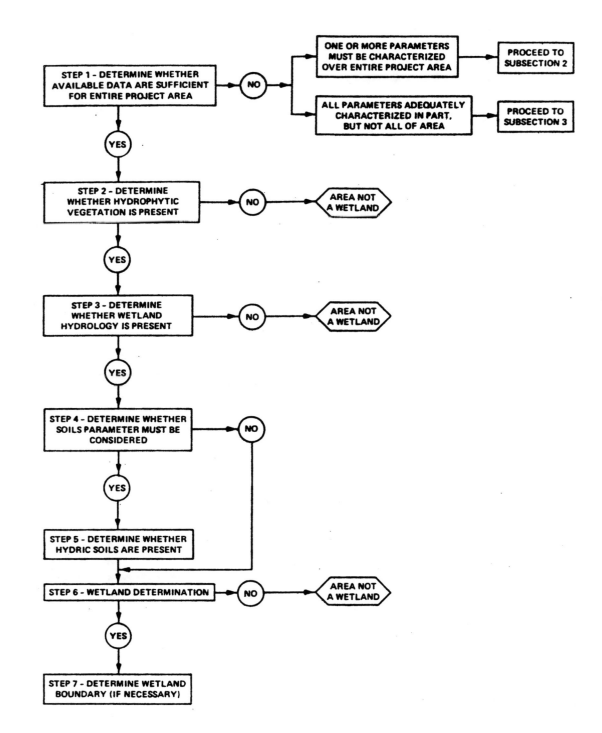

Figure 4.1. **Flowchart of Steps Involved in Making a Wetland Determination When an Onsite Inspection is Unnecessary** (From *Corps of Engineers Wetland Delineation Manual*, 1987).

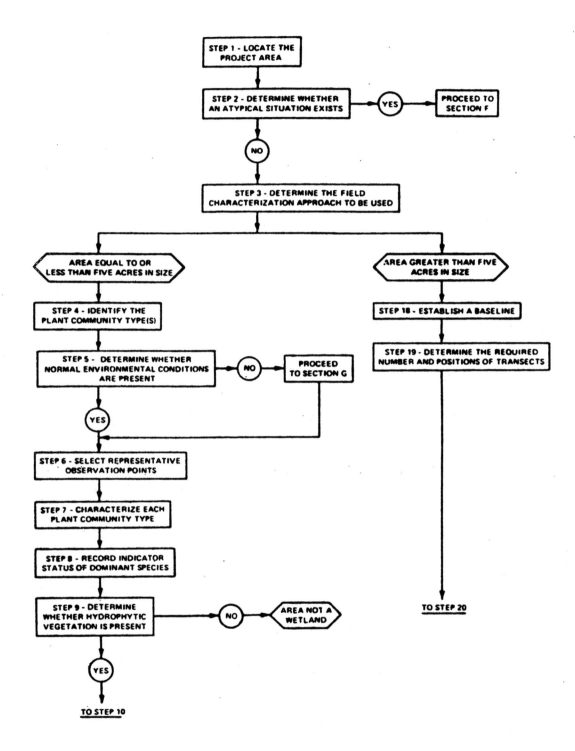

Figure 4.2. **Flowchart of Steps Involved in Making a Routine Wetland Delineation** (From *Corps of Engineers Wetland Delineation Manual*, 1987).

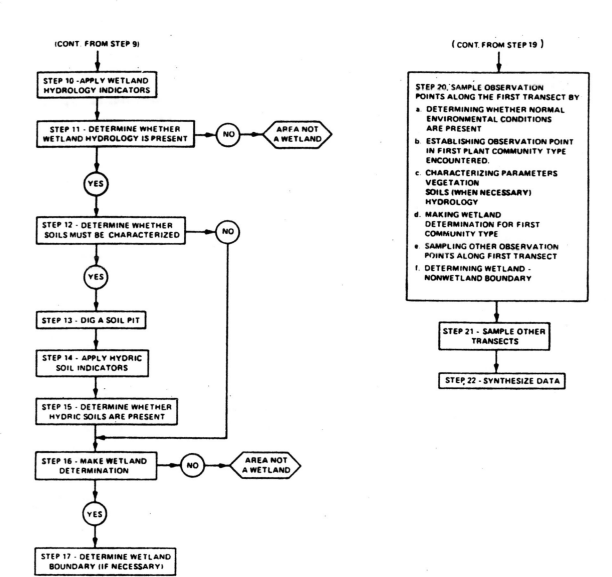

Figure 4.2 (continued)

Comprehensive Determinations

A flow chart illustrating the steps in the comprehensive method is presented in **Figure 4.3**, on the following pages. The 1987 Manual describes the steps for comprehensive determinations in great detail including the required equipment. This method is similar to the Level 2 Routine Method for sites greater than five acres in size. The difference is in the quantitative determination of dominance in the comprehensive method versus the estimated determination of dominance in the Level 2 Routine method. The analysis of soil and hydrology basically the same.

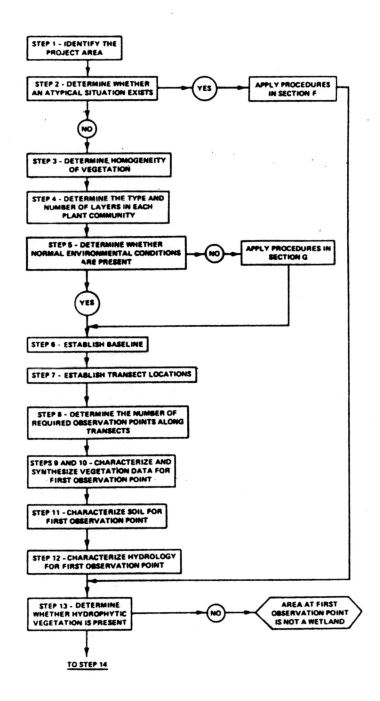

Figure 4.3. **Flowchart of Steps Involved in Making a Comprehensive Wetland Determination** (From *Corps of Engineers Wetlands Delineation Manual*, 1987).

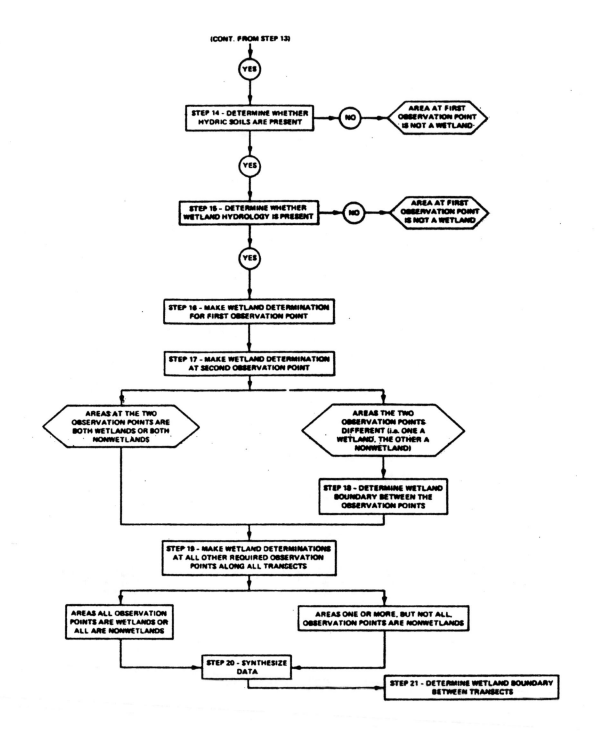

Figure 4.3 (continued)

ATYPICAL SITUATIONS

This method is intended for use when the initial routine of comprehensive investigation determines that positive indicators of one or more of the three parameters are absent due to recent activities of man or natural events. Three specific situations are described in the manual in some detail and are paraphrased below:

- *unauthorized activities* which have resulted in alterations of a wetland (i.e., removal of vegetation, filling of wetlands, or alteration of hydrology through construction of levees or drainage systems).

- *natural events* which may result in the creation or alteration of wetlands, but where certain parameters such as hydric soil indicators have not had sufficient time to develop.

- *man-induced wetlands* including those created intentionally or accidentally, and again, where there has been insufficient time for the development of indicators for the three parameters.

The atypical situation method takes a historical approach for determination in the first two cases, unauthorized activities and natural events. The decision is based on whether positive indicators of the three parameters existed prior to the alteration of the area. Acceptable data sources and procedures are described in a detailed step by step manner for the analysis of vegetation, soils, and hydrology. The procedure sends the investigator back to the appropriate point in the routine or comprehensive method after the historical analysis of the altered parameter(s) is finished.

The procedure for man-induced wetlands is discussed in a separate subsection. This method recognizes that the formation of hydric soil indicators (which may take hundreds of years) lags that of hydrology, which can occur immediately when a berm or levee is constructed, and vegetation which can develop over the course of one or two growing seasons. This is the one case in the 1987 Manual where a wetland determination can be made on the basis of two parameters, vegetation, and hydrology. However, the hydrology causing the presence of the hydrophytic vegetation must be very carefully analyzed prior to a positive determination. Irrigation for example, even if it has been taking place for a long period, does not constitute sufficient hydrology.

PROBLEM AREAS

The problem area procedures recognize that there are certain wetland types where positive indicators of all three parameters may be lacking even under "normal" circumstances due to regional climatic, geologic, or other conditions. Several representative examples of potential problem areas are listed and described in the 1987 Manual. These are listed below:

- wetlands on drumlins
- seasonal wetlands
- prairie wetlands
- vegetated flats

The first three examples represent different wetland types where hydrology may be very difficult to recognize during the drier months of the year. In the case of prairie potholes, during a dry year or cycle the hydrology may be so slight that farmers may actually farm wetlands which would could potentially remove positive indicators of vegetation and soil. The vegetated flats example describes wetland communities where the vegetation consists of annual, obligate wetland plants which would not be present during the nongrowing season. A delineator operating during the nongrowing season could make an erroneous determination unless he or she were familiar with the ecology of the system.

The prescribed methodology in this section is not as clear as that in the proceeding sections because approach is largely dependent on the type of system being investigated. Basic knowledge of the community type in question is listed as one of the three sources of evidence for determination. This may be provided by the delineator as well as local expertise from universities or other sources. Available information and field data are the others. The final decision rests on the conclusion that wetlands are or are not "normally present" during the growing season.

REGULATORY GUIDANCE LETTERS

The U.S. Army Corps of Engineers periodically issues Regulatory Guidance Letters ("RGLs" or, sometimes "Regals") which are published in the Federal Register. These letters, which range from clarifications of existing policy to statements of new policy in response to new developments within the wetland industry or as a result of court decisions, generally address permitting issues. Occasionally Regulatory Guidance Letters are issued which pertain specifically to wetland delineation protocol and technique. Most Regulatory Guidance Letters list an effective date and an expiration date, however, they are normally in effect indefinitely regardless of the expiration date.

Two significant Regulatory Guidance Letters regarding wetland delineation were issued on August 14, 1990 and March 6, 1992. The August 14, 1990 letter established a specific time limitation for the validity of wetland delineations verified by the appropriate regulatory agency. The time standard established in this guidance letter was three years from the date of the official letter verifying the delineation. The March 6, 1992 letter provides "additional clarification and guidance concerning the application for the 1987 Manual. This three-page memorandum simply embellishes specific procedural details for the assessment of vegetation, hydrology, and soil parameters during a delineation.

Although the Regulatory Guidance Letters generally address only small details or inconsistencies in the delineation techniques or other regulatory policies, it is important for wetland professionals specializing in delineation and permitting issues to stay abreast of these changes. This can be accomplished by reading the Federal Register or by contacting the U.S. Army Corps of Engineer's Washington, D.C. and requesting copies of the guidance letters (202-272-1782). The Corps publishes the text of all current guidance letters annually in the Federal Register.

CHAPTER FIVE
THE PERMIT REQUIREMENT

JURISDICTIONAL ISSUES

Prior to the enactment of the Clean Water Act in 1972, the Rivers and Harbors Act of 1899 was the only source of federal power to regulate dredging and filling in navigable waters,[8] and to require a permit for the discharge of industrial pollution.[9] Gradually, the Corps's permitting function under the Rivers and Harbors Act of 1899 evolved by the enactment of new statutes and agreements with other federal departments to include the Corps's consideration of other impacts besides simple navigability. Ultimately, this authority included consideration of environmental impacts among other factors when the Corps was deciding whether to issue a Rivers and Harbors Act permit.[10] The evolutionary process led to the enactment of the Federal Water Pollution Control Act Amendments of 1972 (known popularly as the Clean Water Act), including §404,[11] which is used to regulate activities in wetlands because "pollutants" were specifically defined in the Clean Water Act to include "fill

---

[8]   33 U.S.C. §§403, 407.

[9]   *United States v. Republic Steel Corp.*, 362 U.S. 482, 4 L.Ed.2d 903, 80 S.Ct. 884, *reh'g. denied*, 363 U.S. 858, 4 L.Ed.2d 1739, 80 S.Ct. 1605 (1960), on remand, 286 F.2d 875 (7th Cir. Ill. 1961); *United States v. Standard Oil*, 384 U.S. 224, 16 L.Ed.2d 492, 86 S.Ct. 1427 (1966).

[10]   *Zabel v. Tabb*, 430 F.2d 199 (5th Cir. 1970), *cert. denied*, 401 U.S. 910, 27 L.Ed.2d 808, 91 S.Ct. 873 (1971).

[11]   33 U.S.C §1344. The Clean Water Act has been amended twice since 1972, in 1977 and 1987, but no changes were made to §404.

material".[12]

The stated goal of the Clean Water Act is ". . . to restore and maintain the chemical, physical, and biological integrity of waters of the United States through the control of discharges of dredged or fill material".[13] To accomplish this halcyon goal, having determined that a geographical area is a "waters of the United States",[14] the Clean Water Act thus prohibits discharging pollutants from a point source into "waters of the United States" without a permit, the purpose of the permit being to control pollution.[15] The Environmental Protection Agency is empowered to grant pollutant discharge permits.[16] Because of its historic role in dredging and fill activities under the Rivers and Harbors Act, the Corps has been given a special duty under the Clean Water Act: the Corps may grant the permits[17] to discharge "dredged and fill material into the navigable waters at specified disposal sites", wetlands among them.[18] Thus, if it is

---

[12]   "The term 'pollutant' means dredged spoil, solid waste, incinerator residue, sewage, garbage, sewage sludge, munitions, chemical wastes, biological materials, radioactive materials, heat, wrecked or discarded equipment, rock, sand, cellar dirt and industrial, municipal, and agricultural waste discharged into water. . . .33 U.S.C. §1362(6).

[13]   40 C.F.R. §230.1(a).

[14]   See *United States v. Mills*, 817 F.Supp. 1546 (N.D.Fla. 1993), *aff'd.* 36 F.3d 1052 (11th Cir. Fla. 1994).

[15]   33 U.S.C. §1311.

[16]   33 U.S.C. §1342. See also *Orange Environment, Inc. v. County of Orange*, 811 F.Supp. 926 (S.D.N.Y. 1993), *aff'd sub nom. Orange Env't. v. Orange County Legislature*, 2 F.3d 1235 (2d Cir. N.Y. 1993).

[17]   Although the Corps actually grants the permits, the Environmental Protection Agency retains an oversight function and may, in certain circumstances, overrule the Corps's permit decision. See *Memorandum of Agreement Between the Department of the Army and the Environmental Protection Agency Concerning Determination of the Geographic Jurisdiction of the Section 404 Program and the Application of Exceptions Under Section 404(f) of the Clean Water Act* (January 19, 1989) (hereinafter the "Jurisdiction MOA").

[18]   33 U.S.C. §1344(a). This statute is commonly known as, and will be hereinafter referred to as "§404". See also *United States v. Mills, supra.*

determined that the area in question is a wetland,[19] a permit to discharge dredged or fill material will be necessary unless one of the exempt activities is contemplated or the activity fits either a general or nationwide permit.

In addition, some assertions of jurisdiction over wetlands with less conspicuous connections either to navigable waters or interstate commerce have been upheld by the courts. In particular, so-called "artificially created wetlands", those which were not naturally present before but resulted from some Man-made activity, are subject to Clean Water Act jurisdiction,[20] as are seasonal wetlands[21] and isolated wetlands.[22]

---

[19]   Even though the Clean Water Act never uses the word "wetlands", their inclusion in the regulatory scheme as "waters of the United States" is found in the regulations and case law. The Corps initially took the position that the extent of its permitting authority under the Clean Water Act was coterminous with its traditional authority under the Rivers and Harbors Act, namely navigable waters, including waters subject to the ebb and flow of the tides, waters which are or have been used to transport interstate commerce, tidal flats under navigable waters, and the natural meandering of rivers. A citizens suit forced the expansion of the Corps's regulatory definition of "waters of the United States" to include wetlands. *Natural Resources Defense Council v. Callaway*, 392 F.Supp. 685 (D.D.C. 1975). See also 52 ALR Fed. 788, §3. Now, the Corps's regulations are rife with references to wetlands. 33 C.F.R. §§ 328.3(a)(2), 328.3(a)(3), and 328.3(a)(7). These new regulations were specifically upheld in *United States v. Riverside Bayview Homes*, 474 U.S. 121, 88 L.Ed.2d 419, 106 S.Ct. 455 (1985). Usually the property owner conducts the wetland delineation, most likely using a consultant with specialized knowledge in this area. If the Corps or the Environmental Protection Agency determines that a wetland is present, there is not much chance that a court will overturn the decision, particularly if a permit is also issued, but, if they decide that a wetland is not present, judicial review is available. *Golden Gate Audubon Society v. U.S. Army Corps of Engineers*, 717 F.Supp. 1417 (N.D.Cal. 1988); *National Wildlife Federation v. Hanson*, 623 F.Supp. 1539 (E.D.N.C. 1985).

[20]   *Leslie Salt Co. v. United States*, 896 F.2d 354 (9th Cir. Cal. 1990), *cert. denied*, 498 U.S. 1126, 112 L.Ed.2d 1194, 111 S.Ct. 1089 (1991); *United States v. DeFelice*, 641 F.2d 1169 (5th Cir. La. 1981), *cert. denied*, 454 U.S. 940, 70 L.Ed.2d 247, 102 S.Ct. 474 (1981); *Swanson v. United States*, 789 F.2d 1368 (9th Cir. Idaho 1986); *United States v. Ft. Pierre*, 747 F.2d 464 (8th Cir. S.D. 1984); *Weiszmann v. District Engineer, U.S. Army Corps of Engineers*, 526 F.2d 1302 (5th Cir. Fla. 1976); *Track 12, Inc. v. District Engineer*, 618 F.Supp. 448 (D.Minn. 1985); *United States v. Bradshaw*, 541 F.Supp. 880 (D.Md. 1981).

[21]   *Quivira Mining Co. v. EPA*, 765 F.2d 126 (10th Cir. 1985), *cert. denied*, 474 U.S. 1055, 88 L.Ed.2d 769, 106 S.Ct. 791 (1986); *United States v. Phelps Dodge Corp.*, 391 F.Supp. 1181 (D.Ariz. 1975).

[22]   The courts do not view isolated wetlands jurisdiction with particular favor, especially when the government argues that its basis of jurisdiction is the Commerce Clause because the isolated wetland

(continued...)

ACTIVITIES REQUIRING A PERMIT

While most activity occurring in a wetland, one which places solid matter in the wetland, will be subject to the permit requirement, it is important to remember that the §404 does not apply to prohibit all activities which may occur in a wetland, but only to the discharge of dredged and fill material from a "point source", even though these other activities may have an equally deleterious effect on wetlands, even to the point of destroying them. The definition of "point source" as

> "any discernible, confined, and discrete conveyance, including but not limited to any pipe, ditch, channel, tunnel, conduit, well, discrete fissure, container, rolling stock, concentrated animal feeding operation, or vessel or other floating craft, from which pollutants may be discharged" (but not agricultural stormwater discharges and return flows from irrigated agriculture)[23]

has evoked some controversy. Even the exclusion of agricultural stormwater discharges is subject to doubt given new knowledge of the source of nitrates in confined lakes and bays.[24]

Such other unprohibited activities might include the dredging activity itself[25]

---

[22](...continued)
may be used as bird or wildlife habitat. *Tabb Lakes Ltd. v. United States*, 10 F.3d 796 (Fed.Cir. 1993); *Hoffman Homes, Inc. v. United States Environmental Protection Agency, supra.* But see *Leslie Salt Co. v. United States, supra.*; *Utah by Division of Parks & Recreation v. Marsh*, 740 F.2d 799 (10th Cir. Utah 1984); *Palila v. Hawaii Department of Land & Natural Resources*, 471 F.Supp. 985 (D.Haw. 1979), *aff'd*, 639 F.2d 495 (9th Cir. Haw. 1981).

[23]   33 U.S.C. §1362(14).

[24]   Stormwater drainage has traditionally been considered a "non-point source", however, if fill material is placed in such a manner as to increase the likelihood than rainwater will carry the fill into a wetland, then jurisdiction has been asserted successfully. *Sierra Club v. Abston Construction Co.*, 620 F.2d 41 (5th Cir. Ala. 1980).

[25]   But see *Salt Pond Assocs. v. Army Corps of Engineers*, 815 F.Supp. 766 (D.Del. 1993).

(so long as there is no discharge of the excavated material), drainage activities,[26] vegetation destruction including landclearing or mowing (so long as no mechanized equipment is used in wetlands),[27] and pile driving.[28]

Initially there was some disagreement between the Corps and the Environmental Protection Agency over what constituted a discharge of "fill material" as defined in the Corps's Clean Water Act regulations at 33 C.F.R. §323.2(k). The Corps took the position that its jurisdiction extended over discharges of fill material which are intended to replace an aquatic area or change the bottom elevation of a water body. The Environmental Protection Agency took the position that all solid waste discharges, regardless of their intent or effect, were covered by §404. To resolve their conflict, the Corps and the Environmental Protection Agency entered into a "*Memorandum of Agreement . . . Concerning Regulation of Discharges of Solid Waste Under the Clean*

---

[26]   *Save Our Community v. U.S. Environmental Protection Agency*, 971 F.2d 1155 (5th Cir. Tex. 1992); *Orleans Audubon Society v. Lee*, 742 F.2d 901 (5th Cir. La. 1984), *reh'g. denied en banc*, 750 F.2d 69 (5th Cir. La. 1984). A drained area may still be considered a wetland because of the "normal circumstances" provision of the definition, i.e. if the area under normal circumstances is a wetland, then any drainage will not destroy jurisdiction over it. A further caution remains that discharges of fill material into drained wetlands may require a §404 permit. The Corps will look to the effect on the wetland of the fill so as to exclude minor discharges as part of a dredging operation, which do not necessarily affect a wetland, and discharges, no matter how small, which do affect the wetland. The Corps has proposed a regulation on this subject to the question is still open as to how long an area must remain dry after drainage in order to avoid jurisdiction. See also "Recapture Provision", below.

[27]   Avoyelles Sportmen's League v. Marsh, 715 F.2d 897 (5th Cir. La. 1983); Save Our Wetlands, Inc. v. Sands, 711 F.2d 634 (5th Cir. 1983). See also 52 ALR Fed. 788, Supp. §5; Regulatory Guidance Letter, No. 90-5, *Landclearing Activities Subject to Section 404 Jurisdiction*, July 18, 1990; *Salt Pond Association v. Army Corps of Engineers*, 815 F.Supp. 766 (D.Del. 1993)(Corps does *not* have jurisdiction to regulate dredging because Regulatory Guidance Letter 90-5 was not issued in accordance with the federal Administrative Procedure Act).

[28]   Pile driving can go too far. The Corps will assert §404 jurisdiction over pilings on a site-specific basis when they are placed so close together that they effectively replace "an aquatic area with dry land or [change] the bottom elevation of the waterbody. Pilings may have this function or effect when they are placed so as to facilitate sedimentation, or are placed so densely that they in effect displace a substantial percentage of the water in the project area." Regulatory Guidance Letter, *Applicability of Section 404 to Pilings*, No. 90-8 (December 14, 1990).

Water Act".[29] Now a discharge will be considered "fill material" under four circumstances, and thus subject to Corps jurisdiction, if

    (1)   "[t]he discharge has as its primary purpose or has as one principle purpose of multi-purposes to replace a portion of the waters of the United States with dry land or to raise the bottom elevation", or

    (2)   "[t]he discharge results from activities such as road construction or other activities where the material to be discharged is generally identified with construction-type activities.", or

    (3)   "[a] principal effect of the discharge is physical loss or physical modification of waters of the United States, including smothering of aquatic life or habitat.", or

    (4)   "[t]he discharge is heterogeneous in nature and of the type normally associated with sanitary landfill discharges".[30]

The Environmental Protection Agency retained jurisdiction over a discharge "in a liquid, semi-liquid, or suspended form or if it is a discharge of solid material of a homogeneous nature normally associated with single industry wastes . . . including placer mining wastes, phosphate mining wastes, titanium mining wastes, sand and gravel wastes, fly ash, and drilling muds".[31]

GENERAL PERMITS

Section 404(e) of the Clean Water Act authorizes the Corps "after notice and opportunity for public hearing" to issue "general permits on a state, regional, or

---

[29]   51 Fed.Reg. 8871 (March 14, 1986).

[30]   *Id.*

[31]   *Id.*

nationwide basis for any category of activities involving discharges of dredged or fill material if (the Corps) determines that such activities in such category are

(1)   similar in nature and similar in their impact on water quality and the aquatic environment;

(2)   will cause only minimal cumulative adverse effects when performed separately; and,

(3)   will have only minimal cumulative adverse effect on water quality and the aquatic environment.[32]

In the Corps's regulations the purpose of these "general permits", like "nationwide permits" discussed below, is "to allow certain activities to occur with little, if any, delay or paperwork".[33]

The purpose of the "general permit" program is to eliminate the need for a permit application if the activity is one covered by the general permit. In a *Section 404 Enforcement Memorandum of Agreement Procedures Regarding the Applicability of Previously-Issued Corps Permits*, the Corps and Environmental Protection Agency agreed that "the Corps will be responsible for determining whether an alleged illegal discharge of dredged or fill material is authorized under an individual or general permit".[34] When the Environmental Protection Agency becomes aware of an alleged illegal discharge, it has agreed to "contact the appropriate Corps district and request a determination as to whether the discharge is authorized by an individual or general

---

[32]   33 U.S.C. §1344(e)(1). See also 40 C.F.R. §230.7(a), part of the *Guidelines*, and *Abenaki Nation of Mississquoi v. Hughes*, 805 F.Supp. 234 (D.Vt. 1992), *aff'd*. 990 F.2d 729 (2d Cir. Vt. 1993), holding that a creation of compensatory wetlands as part of a project already authorized by a general permit is not itself a "discharge" requiring a permit.

[33]   33 C.F.R. §320.1(a)(3).

[34]   *Section 404 Enforcement Memorandum of Agreement Procedures Regarding the Applicability of Previously-Issued Corps Permits*, January 19, 1989.

permit".[35] A Corps determination, which must be made within either two or ten working days depending upon how much information the Environmental Protection Agency gives it, that the discharge is authorized or unauthorized is a final enforcement decision.[36] Nonetheless, if the Environmental Protection Agency either does not receive a timely Corps determination or "reasonably believes that such discharge is not authorized", the Environmental Protection Agency may take "immediate enforcement action against the discharger when necessary to minimize impacts to the environment".[37] The Environmental Protection Agency still has to contact the Corps in any event and, if the Corps finds that the discharge was authorized, that, too, is a "final determination".[38] In order to find out what kinds of activities in wetlands have been authorized in which states or regions, it is necessary to contact the local Corps division or district office directly.

NATIONWIDE PERMITS

The Corps's regulations authorize it to issue, reissue, modify, suspend, revoke—either in whole or for specific geographical areas, classes of activities, or classes of waters, or propose regional conditions to thirty-six "Nationwide Permits" (hereinafter "NWPs")[39] as long as thirteen general, and nine "Section 404 Only",

---

[35]   *Id*. at ¶3.

[36]   *Id*. at ¶4 and 5.

[37]   *Id*. at ¶6. A "final determination" becomes important in issues regarding ripeness of a permit decision for judicial review. See Chapter 9, below.

[38]   *Id*.

[39]   33 C.F.R. §330.6.

conditions are met.[40] This program is so generous in its coverage that only thirteen of the thirty-six NWPs require a special notice procedure[41] before commencing the activity. The remainder of the NWPs are technically self-executing though wisdom and practice teach that the Corps should be contacted whenever any activity will be conducted in a wetland just to make certain that a NWP applies.[42]

Coastal zone management consistency determinations[43] and state water quality certifications remain necessary though that procedure may itself by eliminated by the applicability of the NWP in the individual state.[44] If the state issues a water quality certification with conditions on a state-wide or regional basis, then under the Corps's regulations, the conditions will become part of the NWP in that particular state or region, unless the Corps determines that the conditions do not comply with other Corps regulations, in which case the water quality certification is deemed denied until the state issues a certification or waives its right to do so.[45]

NWPs frequently provide a safe harbor in violation cases since the Corps is authorized to terminate an enforcement proceeding with an after-the-fact NWP if all of the terms and conditions of the NWP have been satisfied either before or after the activity has been accomplished.[46] Nonetheless, the Corps retains discretionary

---

[40]   33 C.F.R. §330.6 and Appendix A to 33 C.F.R. §330.

[41]   *Id.*

[42]   33 C.F.R. §330.6(a)(1) allows a landowner to request and receive a confirmation from the Corps that the proposed activity complies with an NWP.

[43]   33 C.F.R. §330.4(d).

[44]   33 C.F.R. §330.4(c).

[45]   33 C.F.R. §§330.4(c)(2) and (3). Other federal statutes, such as the Endangered Species Act and the National Historic Preservation Act, remain applicable although there are provisions in 33 C.F.R. §§330.4(a), 330.4(d), 330.4(f) and Appendix A to §330, Subpart C, "Nationwide Permits". See also *Vieux Carre Property Owners, Residents & Assocs. v. Brown*, 875 F.2d 453 (5th Cir. La. 1989), *cert. denied* 493 U.S. 1020, 107 L.Ed.2d 739, 110 S.Ct. 720 (1990).

[46]   33 C.F.R. §§330.1© and 330.6(e).

authority,[47] even in cases in which an NWP would appear to apply, to suspend, modify, or revoke an NWP authorization if the Corps determines that the activity would have more than a minimal individual or cumulative net adverse effect on the environment, or that the activity is contrary to the public interest.[48] In these instances, the Corps must instruct the landowner to apply for either a general or individual permit. Another useful regulation is that two or more different NWPs may be applied to a single and complete project (but the same NWP may not be applied more than once to a single and complete project).[49] In addition, under certain conditions, an NWP may be applied to a portion of a larger project while the individual permit is being evaluated on a different portion.[50]

Some of the NWPs require a delineation. In these cases, if the Corps determines that the adverse effects are more than minimal, the Corps may either require an individual permit or allow the landowner to propose mitigation measures.[51] If the landowner bites the bullet and proposes mitigation along with the original notification, the Corps may consider the mitigation proposal at the same time it is deciding whether the adverse effects are minimal, thus enhancing the chances of permit issuance.[52] Nonetheless, the Corps is supposed to consider the availability of NWPs in reviewing all permit applications, and thus may contact a landowner that an activity could comply with an NWP after reasonable project modifications and/or activity-specific

---

[47]   See also 33 C.F.R. §330.1(d).

[48]   33 C.F.R. §§330.4 and 330.5.

[49]   33 C.F.R. §330.6(c).

[50]   33 C.F.R. §330.6(d).

[51]   33 C.F.R. §330.1(e)(3); Appendix A to §330, Subpart C, "Nationwide Permit Conditions", ¶13(f).

[52]   33 C.F.R. §330.1(e).

conditions.[53]

We have provided the numbers of each of the NWPs in this text because they are frequently referred to by their numbers alone, e.g "Nationwide 18" to cover a minor discharge, or "Nationwide 26" to cover discharges causing the loss of ten acres or less. The thirty-six NWPs are:

№ 1: Aids To Navigation: This NWP permits the placement of Coast Guard-approved aids to navigation and regulatory markers so long as they are installed in accordance with the requirements of the U.S. Coast Guard.

№ 2: Structures In Artificial Canals: This NWP permits the construction of structures in artificial canals within principally residential developments where the connection of the canal to a navigable water has been previously authorized.

№ 3: Maintenance: Repair, rehabilitation, or replacement of any previously authorized (or constructed prior to the requirement for authorization) currently serviceable structure or fill provided that the structure or fill is not put to a different use than the use specified or contemplated in the original permit or its most recent modification. "Currently serviceable" means that the structure or fill is useable as is or with some maintenance but not so degraded as to essentially require reconstruction, except when the structure has been destroyed by a storm, flood, fire, or other discrete event. Minor, necessary deviations in the structure's configuration or the filled area due to changes in materials or construction techniques are authorized by this NWP so long as the environmental impacts are minimal. However, this NWP does not authorize maintenance dredging or beach restoration.

№ 4: Fish And Wildlife Harvesting, Enhancement, and Attraction Devices and Activities: This NWP allows the placement of and activities associated with pound

---

[53]   33 C.F.R. §330.1(f).

nets, crab and lobster traps, eel pots, duck blinds, clam and oyster digging, and other fish and wildlife harvesting devices and activities. This NWP does not, however, authorize impoundments for the culture or holding of motile species.

№ 5: Scientific Measurement Devices: This NWP allows the placement and associated activity in connection with staff and tide gauges, water recording and quality devices, and similar scientific structures. This NWP requires notification prior to commencement of the activity.

№ 6: Survey Activities: Survey activities, which may include core sampling, seismic exploratory operations, and the plugging of seismic shot holes and other exploratory bore holes, are authorized by this NWP. However, the drilling of exploratory-type bore holes for oil and gas test is not authorized although the plugging of these holes is. The discharge of drilling muds may, nonetheless, require a permit.

№ 7: Outfall Structures: Outfall structures and associated intake structures are authorized under this NWP provided that the effluent from the outfall has been permitted or specifically exempted under the National Pollution Discharge Elimination System[54] and that the Corps has determined that the cumulative adverse environmental effects of the structure itself are minimal. This NWP also requires prior notification. Intake structures alone are not authorized by this NWP; only those intakes directly associated with outfalls are covered.

№ 8: Oil And Gas Structures: Structures for the exploration, production, and transportation of oil, gas, and minerals on the outer continental shelf within areas leased for such purposes by the Department of Interior, Mineral Management Service, are authorized by this NWP provided that theses structures are not placed within the limits of any designated shipping safety fairway or traffic separation scheme.

---

[54]   See §402 of the Clean Water Act; §405 of the Water Quality Act.

№9: Structures In Fleeting and Anchorage Areas: Structures placed in U.S. Coast Guard-established anchorages or fleeting areas to facilitate the moorage of vessels are authorized by this NWP.

№ 10: Single-Boat Mooring Buoys: This NWP authorizes the placement of non-commercial, single-boat mooring buoys.

№ 11: Temporary Recreational Structures: Except at Corps reservoirs, temporary buoys, markers, and small floating docks placed for recreational uses such as water-skiing and boat racing, are authorized by this NWP provided they are removed within thirty days after their use has been discontinued. If the markers or buoys are placed in a Corps reservoir, the reservoir manager much approve each marker or buoy individually.

№12: Utility Line Backfill and Bedding: The discharge of material for backfill or bedding for utility lines, including outfall and intake structures, is authorized by this NWP provided there is no change to the pre-construction bottom contours (meaning that the bottom contours must be restored. This NWP defines a "utility line" as a pipe or pipeline for the transportation of any gaseous, liquid, liquefiable, or slurry substance, for any purpose, and any cable, line, or wire for the transmission for any purpose of electrical energy, telephone and telegraph messages, and radio and television communication. Even so, if the utility line and outfall and intake structures are located in navigable waters, then a §10 Rivers and Harbors Act of 1899 permit will still be required. There are limitations on the location of sidecast material and the length of time it may be allowed to remain outside its original location.

№13: Bank Stabilization: Bank stabilization activities for erosion prevention are authorized provided that the fill is the minimum amount necessary, the activity is less than 500 feet long and limited to less than an average of one cubic yard per running

foot placed along the bank within waters of the United States, the fill is not placed in a wetland area, does not impair surface water flow into and out of any wetland area, will not itself be eroded, and the activity is a single and complete project. Upon notice to the Corps, bank stabilization activities greater than 500 feet long or with a greater than one cubic yard per running foot average amount of fill may be authorized if the Corps determines that the impacts are minimal.

Nº 14: Road Crossing Fills: This NWP authorizes fills for roads crossing waters of the United States provided that the fill is the minimum width necessary for the actual crossing, the fill is limited to no more than one-third of an acre of which no more than 200 linear feet can occur in a wetland, the fill is designed to prevent the restriction of, and to withstand, expected high flows and to prevent the restriction of low flows and the movement of aquatic organisms. If the fill is to be placed in a wetland, prior notification is required.

Nº 15: U.S. Coast Guard Approved Bridges: Discharges of dredged or fill material incidental to construction of bridges across navigable waters, including cofferdams, abutments, foundation seals, piers, and temporary construction and access fills are authorized by this NWP provided that the discharge has been authorized by the U.S. Coast Guard as part of the bridge permit. Causeways and approach fills are not authorized by this NWP and will require either a regional or individual permit.

Nº 16: Return Water From Upland Contained Disposal Areas: The return water from an upland, contained dredged material disposal area is authorized even though its disposal occurs on the upland. The dredging activity itself will require a §10 of the Rivers and Harbors Act of 1899 permit if it is located in navigable waters.

Nº 17: Hydropower Projects: Fills associated with small hydropower projects at existing reservoirs are authorized by this NWP provided that the project which includes the fill is either licensed or exempt from licensing by the Federal Energy Regulatory Commission, has a total generating capacity of not more than 5000 KW, and the permittee notifies the Corps.

№ 18: Minor Discharges: Discharges of less than twenty-five cubic yards of dredged or fill material into waters of the United States other than wetlands as part of a single and complete project are authorized by this NWP provided that the discharge does not cause the loss of more than one-tenth of an acre of filled area plus the affected area. For fills of greater than ten cubic yards, the Corps must be notified, including a delineation, prior to commencing the activity. In any event, the discharge must be part of a single and complete project and not placed for the purpose of stream diversion.

№19: Minor Dredging: Dredging of no more than twenty-five cubic yards from navigable waters of the United States as part of a single and complete project are authorized by this NWP except for dredging or degradation through siltation of coral reefs, submerged aquatic vegetation, anadromous fish spawning areas, or wetlands, or the connection of canals to navigable waters of the United States.

№ 20: Oil Spill Cleanup: Activities for the containment and cleanup of oil and hazardous substances which are subject to the National Oil and Hazardous Substances Pollution Contingency Plan are authorized by this NWP provided that the Regional Response Team concurs with the proposed containment and cleanup action.

№21: Surface Coal Mining Activities: Activities associated with surface coal mining are authorized by this NWP provided that they were authorized by the Department of the Interior, Office of Surface Mining or by the State under programs approved under the Surface Mining Control and Reclamation Act of 1977, and the Corps has received prior notification including a delineation.

Nº 22: Removal Of Wrecked Vessels: Temporary structures and minor discharges of dredged or fill material which are required for the removal of wrecked, abandoned, or disabled vessels, or the removal of man-made obstructions to navigation are authorized by this NWP with the exceptions of maintenance dredging, shoal removal, or river bank snagging.

Nº 23: Approved Categorical Exclusions: Activities which are undertaken, assisted, authorized, regulated, funded, or financed, in whole or in part, by another Federal agency or department are authorized by this NWP. The "other federal agency or department" must have determined that the activity is categorically excluded from environmental documentation because it is included in a category of actions which neither individually or cumulatively have a significant effect on the human environment. Further, the Corps must have been notified of and concurs with the federal agency's or department's application for the categorical exclusion. The Corps is also required to solicit comments before concurring.

Nº 24: State Administered Section 404 Programs: Any activity permitted by a State administering its own program under §404 of the Clean Water Act is automatically permitted under §10 of the Rivers and Harbors Act.

Nº 25: Structural Discharges: Discharges of concrete into tightly sealed forms or cells are authorized by this NWP provided that the concrete is used as a structural member for standard pile supported structures or linear projects, but not used to support buildings, homes, parking areas, storage areas, or other such structures.

Nº 26: Headwaters and Isolated Waters Discharges: Discharges of dredged or fill material into headwaters or isolated waters provided the discharge does not cause the loss of more than ten acres of waters of the United States are authorized by this NWP but it requires prior notification and a delineation for losses of more than one acre. The acreages include the areas to be filled as well as the areas affected as a result of the project and special rules apply to subdivisions.

Nº27: Wetland and Riparian Restoration and Creation Activities: Activities associated with the restoration of altered and degraded non-tidal wetlands, riparian areas and the creation of wetlands and riparian areas in accordance with certain conditions are authorized by this NWP. This NWP does not, however, allow the conversion of natural wetlands to a different aquatic use such as the creation of waterfowl impoundments where a forested wetland previously existed.

Nº 28: Modifications of Existing Marinas: This NWP authorizes reconfiguration of existing marinas but not dredging or expansion.

Nºs 29, 30, and 31 have been reserved.

Nº 32: Completed Enforcement Actions: Any structure, work, or discharge undertaken in accordance with, or remaining in place in compliance with a court order or settlement agreement in an enforcement action under the Clean Water Act or the Rivers and Harbors Act of 1899.

Nº33: Temporary Construction, Access and Dewatering: Temporary structures for construction purposes are authorized under this NWP so long as the permanent activity was previously authorized and the Corps receives prior notification. Temporary fill must be removed upon completion.

Nº34: Cranberry Production Activities: Upon prior notification to the Corps, cranberry production operations may disturb up to a cumulative total of ten acres.

Nº 35: Maintenance Dredging of Existing Basins: Accumulated sediment may be removed from existing marina basins, canals, and boat slips provided the dredged material is disposed of at an upland site and proper siltation controls are used.

N⁰36: Boat Ramps: Up to fifty cubic yards of concrete, rock, crushed stone or gravel may be discharged to construct a boat ramp no wider than 20 feet wide so long as it is not in a wetland.

N⁰37: Emergency Watershed Protection and Rehabilitation: Soil Conservation Service and Forest Service activities may complete exigent work upon prior notice to the Corps.

N⁰ 38: Cleanup of Hazardous and Toxic Waste: Upon prior notification to the Corps (and a delineation in the case of wetlands), government-conducted cleanup and remedial action is authorized, but not the creation of new, or the expansion of existing, disposal sites.

N⁰ 39 has been reserved.

N⁰40: Farm Buildings: Discharges of the minimum amount necessary, but in no event more than one acre, to construct foundations and building pads of farm buildings in farmed wetlands (but not prairie potholes, playa lakes, or vernal pools).

In order to validate the foregoing thirty-six NWP's, the regulations impose compliance with thirteen additional "general" conditions. Those additional general conditions are:

(1)   That the activity may not cause more than a minimal adverse effect on navigation;

(2)   That the structure or fill will be properly maintained;

(3)   That appropriate erosion and siltation controls will be used and maintained during construction;

(4)   That any activity shall not substantially disrupt the movement of indigenous aquatic species unless the primary purpose of the fill is to impound water;

(5)   That heavy equipment must be placed on mats or other measures taken to minimize soil disturbance;

(6)   That the activity complies with regional and case-specific conditions;

(7)   That the activity will not occur in a component of the National Wild and Scenic River System, nor in a river officially designated by Congress as a "study river" for possible inclusion in the System while the river is in an official study status;

(8)   That the activity will not impair reserved tribal rights, including, but not limited to, reserved water rights and treaty fishing and hunting rights;

(9)   That in certain states an individual state water quality certification must be obtained or waived;

(10)   That an individual state coastal zone management consistency concurrence must be obtained or waived in certain states;

(11)   That the activity will not jeopardize a threatened or endangered species as identified under the Endangered Species Act, or destroy or adversely modify the critical habitat of such species, and, if the presence or proximity of endangered species is known, non-Federal permittee must notify the Corps and wait for its approval;

(12)   If the activity may adversely affect historic properties which the National Park Services has listed on, or are or may be eligible for listing on, the National Register of Historic Places, that the permittee shall notify the Corps and wait for its approval; and,

(13)   Where notification is required, that the permittee has complied with the specific notification provisions, including a delineation where required. A proposed mitigation plan may also be submitted with the "Pre-Discharge Notification" or "PDN".

In addition to the above general conditions, nine "Section 404 Only Conditions" apply and must be followed. They are:

(1)   No discharge may occur in proximity with a public water supply intake except for repair purposes;

(2)   No discharge shall occur in areas of concentrated shellfish production except when harvesting;

(3)   No discharge may consist of unsuitable material and must be free from toxic pollutants in toxic amounts;

(4)   Discharges must be minimized or avoided to the maximum extent practicable unless there is a Corps-approved mitigation plan;

(5)   Discharges into spawning areas during spawning season must be avoided to the maximum extent practicable;

(6)   Discharges must not permanently restrict or impede the passage of normal or expected high flows or cause the relocation of water unless the primary purpose of the fill is the impoundment of water;

(7)   Impoundments of water shall not cause adverse impacts caused by the accelerated passage of water and/or the restriction of its flow;

(8)   Discharges into migratory waterfowl breeding areas must be avoided; and

(9)   Temporary fills must be removed and the affected areas returned to their pre-existing condition.

Another less-frequently encountered regulatory exemption exists for dry land which is being artificially irrigated or diked to form a stock or irrigation pond or a swimming or ornamental pool.

In March, 1995, the Corps proposed an additional NWP pursuant to President Clinton's August, 1993 wetland policy. Under this proposed NWP, a landowner could, by the discharge of dredged or fill material, cause an aggregate loss of wetlands of no more than one-half acre for the construction or expansion of a single-family home if he or she notifies the Corps (but not other resource agencies as is required for other

NWP's) and has taken steps to minimize the impact of the discharge so long as the discharge is part of a single and complete project. The landowner could use the proposed NWP only once for all property owned now and in the future. There is no proposed requirement for mitigation or compensation; only that the impact has been minimized. The one-half-acre limitation would include not only the area of direct impact, but also other on- and off-site areas adversely affected by the discharge.

EXEMPT ACTIVITIES

After considering the regulatory exemptions discussed above, there are still six more statutory exemptions to §404's coverage, all of them designed to exclude from jurisdiction routine, essentially commercial activities which have minor impacts on wetlands:[55]

(1)   For discharges of dredged and fill material into wetlands and minor drainage (but not a gradual conversion from wetland to non-wetland) which occur during normal farming, silviculture, and ranching activities (plowing, seeding, cultivating, minor drainage, harvesting for the production of food, fiber, and forest products, or upland soil and water conservation practices) so long as the discharge occurred only in an area which was, at the time of the discharge, part of a legitimate, continuously-operated farming operation.[56] If the farm field has lain fallow long enough

---

[55]   33 U.S.C. §1344(f)(1); But see "Recapture Provision", below, if the impact of these exempt activities is more than minimal. See also *United States v. Akers*, 785 F.2d 814 (9th Cir. Cal. 1986), *cert. denied* 479 U.S. 828, 93 L.Ed.2d 56, 107 S.Ct. 107 (1986); *United States v. Huebner*, 752 F.2d 1235 (7th Cir. Wisc. 1985), *cert. denied*, 474 U.S. 817, 88 L.Ed.2d 50, 106 S.Ct. 62 (1985).

[56]   See Regulatory Guidance Letter, *Clarification of the Phrase "Normal Circumstances" as it*
(continued...)

that it now requires modification of its evolved hydrologic regime
to convert it back to farmland, then the exemption will be lost.[57]

(2)   For the purpose of maintenance of currently serviceable dikes,
dams, levees, groins, riprap, breakwaters, causeways, bridge
abutments or approaches, and transportation structures;[58]

(3)   For the purpose of construction or maintenance of farm or stock
ponds or irrigation ditches;[59]

(4)   For the purpose of construction of temporary sedimentation
basins on a construction site (but not the placement of fill material
into navigable waters);[60]

(5)   For the purpose of construction or maintenance of farm, forest, or
temporary mining roads so long as these roads are constructed
and maintained in such a way as to assure compliance with

---

[56](...continued)
pertains to Cropped Wetlands, No. 90-7 (September 26, 1990).

[57]   33 U.S.C. §1344(f)(1)(A). See also *U.S. v. Larkins*, 852 F.2d 189 (6th Cir. Ky. 1988), *cert. denied*, 489 U.S. 1016, 103 L.Ed.2d 193, 109 S.Ct. 1131 (1989); *U.S. v. Cumberland Farms of Connecticut*, 647 F. Supp. 1166 (D.Mass.), *aff'd*, 826 F.2d 1151 (1st Cir. 1987), *cert. denied*, 489 U.S. 1061, 98 L.Ed.2d 981, 108 S.Ct. 1016 (1988); *U.S. v. Akers, supra.; U.S. v. Huebner, supra.*; *Memorandum for the Field, Clean Water Act Section 404 Regulatory Program and Agricultural Activities*, (May 3, 1990) and the Environmental Protection Agency's regulations at 40 C.F.R. §232.3(c).

[58]   33 U.S.C. §1344(f)(1)(B).

[59]   33 U.S.C. §1344(f)(1)(C). See also Regulatory Guidance Letter, No. 87-7, *Section 404(f)(1)(C) Statutory Exemption for Drainage Ditch Maintenance*, (August 17, 1987).

[60]   33 U.S.C. §1344(f)(1)(D).

§404(f)(2);[61] and,

(6)   Certain state programs.[62]

These specifically enumerated exemptions are not subject to jurisdiction under §301(a) or §402 either.

THE RECAPTURE PROVISION

Even though there are five specific topics of exempt activities, these activities will lose their exempt status if the purpose of the activity is to bring ". . . an area of navigable waters into a use to which it was not previously subject, where the flow or circulation of navigable waters may be impaired, or the reach of such waters is reduced".[63] The essential inquiry is whether the activity is "normal and ongoing" or whether it is truly a "new use", which the Corps concedes requires a "judgment call".[64] A "new use" can readily be found if the activity causes some significant alteration to the area's hydrology.

---

[61]   33 U.S.C. §1344(f)(1)(E). See also Regulatory Guidance Letter, No. 86-3, *Section 404(f)(1) Exemption of Farm and Forest Roads (33 CFR Part 323.4(a)(6))*, April 4, 1986.

[62]   33 U.S.C. §1344(f)(1)(F).

[63]   33 U.S.C. §1344(f)(2). This subsection is commonly referred to as the "recapture provision" because it "recaptures" certain apparently exempt activities and brings them back under the permit requirement. See also Regulatory Guidance Letter, No. 87-9, *Section 404(f)(1)(C) Exemption for Construction or Maintenance of Farm or Stock Ponds* (August 27, 1987); *Bayou Marcus Livestock & Agricultural Co. v. EPA*, 20 Envtl.L.Rep. (Envtl.L.Inst.) 20445 (N.D.Fla. 1989) (§403 of the Rivers and Harbors Act also prohibits unpermitted excavation or fill or alteration of the course, location, condition, and capacity of navigable waters).

[64]   Regulatory Guidance Letter, No. 87-9, *Section 404(f)(1)(C) Exemption for Construction or Maintenance of Farm or Stock Ponds* (August 27, 1987).

CHAPTER SIX
PERMITTING PROCEDURES

The regulations concerning the Corps's authority to issue permits for discharging dredged and fill material into wetlands under the Clean Water Act are found at 33 C.F.R. §§320.1(b)(5) and 320.2(f). Its procedures are set forth in great detail at 33 C.F.R. §325.1. The Corps is also required to follow certain *Guidelines* promulgated by the Environmental Protection Agency in deciding whether to issue or deny a permit.[65]

In addition to these national regulations, because the Corps has traditionally been "a highly decentralized organization"[66], much of the permitting authority has been delegated to the thirty-six district engineers and eleven division engineers. Thus, if a district or division engineer makes a permit decision, if it was made in accordance with the regulations, the decision is final. There is no administrative appeal.[67]

Another manifestation of the Corps's traditional decentralization is that each district engineer should have established local procedures and policies to allow potential applicants to contact the office for pre-application consultation for major projects.[68] The district engineer should "endeavor, at this stage, to provide the potential applicant with all helpful information necessary in pursuing the application, including factors which the Corps must consider in its permit decision making process".[69]

---

[65]   33 C.F.R. §320.2(f); See also "Environmental Protection Agency *Guidelines*", below.

[66]   33 C.F.R. §§320.1(a)(2) and 320.2(f).

[67]   33 C.F.R. §320.1(a)(2). Resort to the federal courts is a disgruntled applicant's only alternative. See Chapter 9, below. However, a disgruntled EPA or U.S. Fish and Wildlife Service may seek "elevation" within the Corps to the Assistant Secretary.

[68]   33 C.F.R. §325.1(b).

[69]   *Id.*

Particularly in the case of potential permit applications which "may involve the preparation of an environmental document", the district engineer should advise the potential permit applicants of the requirements for the permit(s) and the attendant public interest review".[70] Potential applicants should also be aware that even the basic permit application form may have regional variations, thus the potential applicant should obtain an application form from the office of the district in which the wetland lies.[71] There is a $100 filing fee for each permit application when the planned or ultimate purpose of the project is commercial or industrial in nature, and is in support of operations that charge for the production, distribution, or sale of goods or services; the filing fee for non-commercial projects is $10.00.[72]

The application form itself is surprisingly simple; its difficulty lies in supplying the information in the requisite degree of specificity and completeness to satisfy the Corps. First, the applicant must include a complete description of the proposed activity including the necessary maps (including a vicinity map, and bird's-eye view, and a cross section), drawings, sketches or plans sufficient for public notice.[73] Although generation of the public notice is a requirement laid on the Corps, since the information to be contained in the notice must come from the applicant, it is discussed here.

---

[70]   *Id* .

[71]   33 C.F.R. §325.1(c). A sample application form is reprinted as an appendix to 33 C.F.R. §325 but, since local variations are allowed, the better practice is to acquire an application form directly from the Corps district in which the subject property lies.

[72]   33 C.F.R. §325.1(f).

[73]   33 C.F.R. §325.1(d). See also *U.S. Army Corps of Engineers, Regulatory Program: Applicant Information.*

PUBLIC NOTICE AND COMMENT

This regulation requires that the information be included in the public notice be sufficient "to give a clear understanding of the magnitude of the activity to generate meaningful comment".[74] The "meaningful comment" contemplated by the regulation is an evaluation of the "probable impact on the public interest".[75] The Corps is required to state in the public notice fifteen separate items of information as they apply to a §404 permit[76]:

(1) A statement of the applicable statutory authority(ies);

(2) The name and address of the applicant;

(3) The name or title, address and telephone number of the Corps contact person from whom additional information concerning the application may be obtained;

(4) The location of the proposed activity;

(5) A brief description of the proposed activity, its purpose and intended use, including a description of the type of structures, if any, to be erected on fills or pile or float-supported platforms;

(6) A plan and elevation drawing showing the general and specific site location and character of all proposed activities, including the

---

[74] 33 C.F.R. §325.3(a).

[75] *Id.*

[76] 33 C.F.R. §325.3(a) lists these topics as well as a handful of other notice requirements which do not apply to permit applications in wetlands.

size relationship of the proposed structures to the size of the impacted waterway and depth of water in the area;

(7)   A list of other government authorizations obtained or requested by the applicant, including required certifications relative to water quality, coastal zone management, or marine sanctuaries;

(8)   If appropriate, a statement that the activity is a categorical exclusion for purposes of the National Environmental Policy Act;

(9)   A statement of the district engineer's current knowledge on historic properties;

(10)   A statement of the district engineer's current knowledge on endangered species (if the district engineer finds that a proposed activity may affect an endangered or threatened species, he will initiate formal consultation procedures with the U.S. Fish and Wildlife Service or National Marine Fisheries Services[77]);

(11)   A statement on evaluation factors[78];

---

[77]   33 C.F.R. §325.2(b)(5).

[78]   The exact wording of this statement, which is repeated in the regulations at 33 C.F.R. §320.4(a), is included in the regulations: "The decision whether to issue a permit will be based on an evaluation of the probable impact including cumulative impacts of the proposed activity on the public interest. That decision will reflect the national concern both for protection and utilization of important resources. The benefit which reasonably may be expected to accrue from the proposal must be balanced against its reasonably foreseeable detriments. All factors which may be relevant to the proposal will be considered including the cumulative effects thereof; among those are conservation, economics, aesthetics, general environmental concerns, wetlands, historic properties, fish and wildlife values, flood hazards, floodplain values, land use, navigation, shoreline erosion and accretion, recreation, water supply and conservation, water quality, energy needs, safety, food and fiber production, mineral needs, considerations of property ownership and, in general, the needs and welfare

(continued...)

(12)   Any other available information which may assist interested parties in evaluating the likely impact of the proposed activity, if any, on factors affecting the public interest;

(13)   The comment period[79];

(14)   A statement that any person may request, in writing, within the comment period specified in the notice, that a public hearing be held to consider the application provided that the request "state, with particularity, the reasons for holding a public hearing"; and

(15)   for private applications in states with an approved Coastal Zone Management Plan, a statement on compliance with the approved Plan.

The Corps will not issue a public notice until it is satisfied that the initial application is complete. The regulations give the Corps fifteen days from receipt of the application to notify the applicant whether it will require any further information.[80] Once the Corps has collected the information and generated the public notice, it distributes the notice for posting to post offices or other appropriate public places in the

---

[78](...continued)
of the people." 33 C.F.R. §325.3(c)(1). Further, if the activity is to occur in a wetland, the statement must also include an application of the Environmental Protection Agency's *Guidelines*.

[79]   The public notice must be issued within fifteen days of receipt of all information required to be submitted. 33 C.F.R. §§325.2(a)(2) and 325.2(d)(2). The comment period runs from the date of the public notice and should be a "reasonable period of time within which interested parties may express their views" but no more than thirty nor less than fifteen days, determined by the Corps's consideration of (1)mail time and the need for comment from remote areas; (2) comments from similar proposals; and (3) the need for a site visit. 33 C.F.R. §325.2(d)(2). If the Corps believes that the comment period should be extended, it may do so for an additional thirty days.

[80]   33 C.F.R. §325.2(a)(1).

vicinity of the proposed work.[81] Copies of the public notice are also sent to the applicant, appropriate city and county officials, adjoining property owners, appropriate state agencies, appropriate Indian tribes, concerned federal agencies, concerned business and conservation organizations, appropriate River Basin Commissions, appropriate state- and area-wide clearing houses, local news media, and to any other interested party.[82] The Corps is required to keep a record of the list of addresses to whom the notice was sent.[83] In addition, if the Corps receives any interim information which would affect the public's view of the proposal, it must issue a "supplemental, revised, or corrected public notice".[84] The Corps "presumes" that all interested parties will wish to respond to public notices therefore a lack of response will be interpreted as no objection.[85]

CONFLICT RESOLUTION

Having received a complete application and issued a public notice, the applicant then enters the "conflict resolution" stage of the permit procedure which lasts for fifteen to thirty days but may be extended.[86] The Corps is required to acknowledge receipt of all comments and to "consider all comments received in response to the public notice".[87] The Corps must seek the advice and special expertise of other federal

---

[81]   33 C.F.R. §325.3(d)(1).

[82]   *Id.*

[83]   33 C.F.R. §325.3(d)(3).

[84]   33 C.F.R. §325.2(a)(2).

[85]   33 C.F.R. §325.3(d)(3).

[86]   33 C.F.R. §325.2(d)(2).

[87]   33 C.F.R. §325.2(a)(3).

agencies if the comments received render such advice and expertise relevant.[88] Most importantly, the Corps is required to inform the applicant of any comments and to receive "the views of the applicant on a particular issue to make a public interest determination".[89] This step in the process is mandatory and a permit denial may be remanded to the Corps if a court finds that the Corps engaged in secret meetings with objectors to the proposed activity.[90] The applicant is given the option to contact the commentators directly to resolve their objections[91], however, since the Corps is solely responsible to make a permit decision, it may convene a Corps-staffed mediation session between the applicant and the commentators.[92] This part of the permit procedure must be followed diligently by the Corps with delays not to exceed thirty days allowed only upon the request of the applicant.[93]

Unless the Corps determines that issues raised in the comments are "insubstantial" or there is "otherwise no valid interest to be served by a hearing", the Corps may decide that a public hearing is necessary.[94] The decision to hold a hearing

---

[88] *Id.*

[89] *Id.*

[90] *Mall Properties v. Marsh*, 672 F.Supp. 561 (D.Mass. 1987), rejecting remand as an appealable order, 841 F.2d 440 (1st Cir. 1988).

[91] 33 C.F.R. §325.2(a)(3). In fact, the applicant is entitled to contact permit objectors. *Mall Properties, Inc. v. Marsh*, 672 F.Supp. 561 (D.Mass. 1987), *appeal dismissed*, 841 F.2d 440 (1st Cir. Mass. 1988), *cert. denied*, 488 U.S. 848, 102 L.Ed.2d 101, 109 S.Ct. 128 (1988).

[92] 33 C.F.R. §325.2(a)(3).

[93] *Id.*

[94] 33 C.F.R. §§325.2(a)(5) and 327.4(b). The Corps is not required to hold a public hearing nor does due process require one. *AJA Associates v. U.S. Army Corps of Engineers*, 817 F.2d 1070 (3d Cir. 1987). Furthermore, these regulations do not require a full hearing under the federal Administrative Procedure Act. *Buttry v. United States*, 690 F.2d 1170 (5th Cir. 1982), *cert. denied*, 461 U.S. 927, 77 L.Ed.2d 298, 103 S.Ct. 2087 (1983); *Shoreline Assoc. v. Marsh*, 555 F.Supp. 169 (D.Md. 1983), *aff'd without op.*, 725 F.2d 677 (4th Cir. Md. 1984); *National Wildlife Federation v. Marsh*, 568 F.Supp. 985 (D.D.C. 1983); *Nofelco Realty Corp. v. United States*, 521 F.Supp. 458

(continued...)

or not must be made in writing, include the Corps's reasons for its decision, be communicated to all requesting parties, and give at least thirty days' notice of the hearing from the date of the public notice.[95] The Corps is required to hold a hearing "in case of doubt" or it may be ordered to hold one.[96] Parties may be represented by counsel and the presiding officer from the Corps may also have a "legal adviser" present.[97] "Any person" may present oral or written statements, call witnesses, and present "recommendations as to an appropriate decision".[98] Cross-examination of witnesses is not allowed[99]. Although the regulations are silent as to whether the rules of evidence apply, the presiding officer may exclude documentary evidence on the grounds of "redundancy".[100] The hearing must be transcribed verbatim.[101] Following the close of the hearing, an additional comment period of not less than ten days is required.[102] The transcript and all evidence introduced will be made part of the administrative record.[103] The Corps's decision must be in writing.[104]

---

[94](...continued)
(S.D.N.Y. 1981).

[95]   33 C.F.R. §§327.4(b) and 327.11.

[96]   33 C.F.R. §327.4(c).

[97]   33 C.F.R. §§327.6 and 327.7.

[98]   33 C.F.R. §327.8(b).

[99]   33 C.F.R. §327.8(d).

[100]   33 C.F.R. §327.8(f).

[101]   33 C.F.R. §327.8(e).

[102]   33 C.F.R. §327.8(g).

[103]   33 C.F.R. §327.9.

[104]   33 C.F.R. §325.2(a)(6).

ENVIRONMENTAL PROTECTION AGENCY *GUIDELINES*

As the Corps is proceeding in its permit decision, gathering all the information necessary, receiving comments after the public notice, and conducting any public hearing it considers necessary, the Corps is required to determine "the probable effect of the proposed work on the public interest" in conformity with the *Guidelines* established by the Environmental Protection Agency.[105] The Corps can override state and local government zoning or land use decisions but must document the override[106] as well as other agencies' views.[107] Wetlands present a special case of permit decision for the Corps because of the multitude of expressions of policy against their alteration or destruction.[108] In fact, the Corps's regulations require that a §404 permit be denied if the discharge would not comply with the EPA's *Guidelines*.[109]

The *Guidelines* are divided into eight subparts, two of which will be considered

---

[105]   33 C.F.R. §325.2(a)(6).

[106]   33 C.F.R. §§320.4(j)(2), 320.4(j)(4), and 325.2(a)(6).

[107]   33 C.F.R. §§320.4© and 320.4(j)(4); *Sierra Club v. Alexander*, 484 F.Supp. 455 (N.D.N.Y.), *aff'd*, 633 F.2d 206 (2d Cir. N.Y. 1980); *Hart & Miller Islands Area Environmental Group, Inc. v. Corps of Engineers of United States Army*, 505 F.Supp. 732 (D.Md. 1980).

[108]   See e.g., 33 C.F.R. §320.4(b)(1): "Most wetlands constitute a productive and valuable public resource, the unnecessary alteration or destruction of which should be discouraged as contrary to the public interest."; 33 C.F.R. §320.4(b)(4): "No permit will be granted which involves the alteration of wetlands . . . unless the (Corps) concludes . . . that the benefits of the proposed alteration outweigh the damage to the wetlands resource." The Guidelines themselves contain similar admonitions to the permit applicant: "Fundamental to the Guidelines is the precept that dredged or fill material should not be discharged into the aquatic ecosystem, unless it can be demonstrated that such a discharge will not have an unacceptable adverse impact either individually or in combination with known and/or probable impacts of other activities affecting the ecosystems of concern" (40 C.F.R. §230.1(c)) and "From a national perspective, the degradation or destruction of special aquatic sites, such as filling operations in wetlands, is considered to be among the most severe environmental impacts covered by these Guidelines. The guiding principle should be that degradation or destruction of special sites may represent an irreversible loss of valuable aquatic resources."(40 C.F.R. §230.1(d)).

[109]   33 C.F.R. §§320.4(a) and 320.4(b)(4); 40 C.F.R. §230.1(c); See also *Bersani v. U.S. Environmental Protection Agency*, 850 F.2d 36 (2d Cir. N.Y. 1988), *cert. denied*, 489 U.S. 1089, 103 L.Ed.2d 859, 109 S.Ct. 1556 (1989).

in this text: Subpart A, 40 C.F.R. §§230.1-230.7, which outlines general policy, definitions, and procedures to be followed; and, Subpart B, 40 C.F.R. §§230.10-230.12, which outlines restrictions on discharge, factual determinations to be made, and findings of compliance or non-compliance with the general restrictions on discharge.

In applying the *Guidelines* to determine whether a potential discharge may be permitted, the Corps must follow a specific procedure. First, it reviews the restrictions on discharge set forth in 40 C.F.R. §§230.10(a) through (d), then the minimization actions in 40 C.F.R. §§230.70 through 230.77, and then the factual determinations required to be made in 40 C.F.R. §230.11.[110] Next the Corps must determine whether any general permits apply.[111] If no general permits apply, the Corps then must examine "practicable alternatives" to the proposed discharge which are either to not allow the discharge at all, or to permit the discharge but into an alternative aquatic site with potentially less damaging consequences after determining proposed alternative sites by applying certain specific factors listed in 40 C.F.R. §230.10(a).[112] If the Corps decides to permit the discharge, it must then "delineate the candidate disposal site" following

---

[110]   40 C.F.R. §230.5(a).

[111]   40 C.F.R. §230.5(b). This regulation refers the Corps to 40 C.F.R. §230.7, "General Permits", which restates the familiar conditions for issuance of general permits, i.e. (1) that the Corps determine that the activities in the category of activities to be generally permitted are similar in nature and similar in their impact upon water quality and the aquatic environment; (2) that the activities in such category will have only minimal adverse effects when performed separately; and (3) that the activities will have only minimal cumulative adverse effects on water quality and the aquatic environment. Further the Corps, in its evaluation of a potential general permit, must consider the four prohibitions listed in 40 C.F.R. §230.10(b), namely (1) that the discharge may not cause or contribute to violations of any applicable state water quality standard; (2) that the discharge may not violate any applicable toxic effluent standard or prohibition; (3) that the discharge may not jeopardize the continued existence of endangered or threatened species or result in the likelihood of destruction or adverse modification of a critical habitat unless an exemption has been granted; and (4) that the discharge may not violate any requirement imposed to protect any designated marine sanctuary, and to 40 C.F.R. §230.10(c), which states the factors to be considered by the Corps in issuing a general permit, namely that there be no discharge which cause or contribute to significant degradation of waters of the United States. See "Significant Degradation of Water", below.

[112]   40 C.F.R. §230.5(c). See also "Practicable Alternatives", below.

the criteria and evaluations set forth in 40 C.F.R. §230.11(f).[113] Next, following Subpart C, the Corps must determine the potential impacts on the physical and chemical characteristics of the aquatic ecosystem by considering the effects on the substrate,[114] the suspended particulates,[115] the chemistry and physical characteristics of the receiving water,[116] current patterns and water circulation,[117] normal water fluctuations such as daily, seasonal, and annual tidal and flood fluctuations,[118] and existing salinity gradients.[119] The Corps then must evaluate any special or critical characteristics of the candidate disposal site and any surrounding areas which may be affected related to their living communities or human uses following the factors listed in Subparts D, E, and F: potential impacts upon biological characteristics including threatened and endangered

---

[113] 40 C.F.R. §230.5(d).Generally the "mixing zone" between the discharge and the aquatic environment "shall be confined to the smallest practicable zone within each specified disposal site" taking into consideration the type of dispersion determined to be appropriate unless, under "unique environmental conditions" in which widespread dispersion by natural means will not result in significant adverse environmental effects, the discharge may be spread in a very thin layer over a large area. 40 C.F.R. §230.11(f)(1).To make the foregoing determination, the Corps must consider ten factors including the depth of the water at the disposal site; the current velocity, direction, and variability; the degree of turbulence; any stratification attributable to causes such as obstructions, salinity or density profiles; discharge vessel speed and direction if appropriate; the rate of discharge; any ambient concentration of constituents of interest; the dredged material characteristics particularly concentrations of constituents, amount of material, type of material, and settling velocities; the number of discharge actions per unit of time; and any other factors that affect rates and patterns of mixing. 40 C.F.R. §230.11(f)(2). See also Chapter 4, "Wetland Delineation", above.

[114] 40 C.F.R. §§230.5(e) and 230.20.

[115] 40 C.F.R. §230.21.

[116] 40 C.F.R. §230.22.

[117] 40 C.F.R. §230.23.

[118] 40 C.F.R. §230.24.

[119] 40 C.F.R. §230.25.

species,[120] fish, crustaceans, mollusks, and other aquatic organisms in the food web,[121] and other wildlife;[122] potential impacts upon special aquatic sites including sanctuaries and refuges,[123] wetlands,[124] mud flats,[125] vegetated shallows,[126] coral reefs,[127] and riffle and pool complexes;[128] and potential impacts upon human use characteristics including municipal and private water supplies,[129] recreational and commercial fisheries, [130]water-related recreation,[131] aesthetics,[132] and parks, national and historical monuments, national seashores, wilderness areas, research sites, and other similar preserves.[133] Next the Corps will review its factual determinations to ensure that the information meets the requirements of 40 C.F.R. §230.11.[134] The Corps must also evaluate the material to be discharged to determine the possibility of chemical contamination or physical

---

[120] 40 C.F.R. §§230.5(f) and 230.30.

[121] 40 C.F.R. §230.31.

[122] 40 C.F.R. §230.32.

[123] 40 C.F.R. §230.40.

[124] 40 C.F.R. §230.41.

[125] 40 C.F.R. §230.42.

[126] 40 C.F.R. §230.43.

[127] 40 C.F.R. §230.44.

[128] 40 C.F.R. §230.45.

[129] 40 C.F.R. §230.50.

[130] 40 C.F.R. §230.51.

[131] 40 C.F.R. §230.52.

[132] 40 C.F.R. §230.53.

[133] 40 C.F.R. §230.54.

[134] 40 C.F.R. §230.5(g).

incompatibility using the procedures outlined in 40 C.F.R. §§230.60 and 230.61.[135] The Corps must also consider appropriate and practicable changes to the project plan to minimize the environmental impact of the discharge by changing the location of the discharge,[136] changing the material to be discharged,[137] controlling the material after its discharge,[138] changing the method of dispersion,[139] use of appropriate technology, design, and equipment,[140] minimizing the adverse effects of plant and animal populations,[141] minimizing adverse effects on human uses,[142] and other miscellaneous actions in special kinds of projects.[143]

All of these Corps factual determinations, findings of compliance, and minimization actions must be made in writing.[144] Even so, the regulations recognize that some projects may be so minor or routine that a full-blown determination with written findings is not necessary, that "different levels of effort . . . should be associated with varying degrees of impact and require or prepare commensurate documentation".[145]

---

[135] 40 C.F.R. §§230.5(h) and (I).

[136] 40 C.F.R. §§230.5(j) and 230.70.

[137] 40 C.F.R. §230.71.

[138] 40 C.F.R. §230.72.

[139] 40 C.F.R. §230.73.

[140] 40 C.F.R. §230.74.

[141] 40 C.F.R. §230.75.

[142] 40 C.F.R. §230.76.

[143] 40 C.F.R. §§230.77 and 230.5(j).

[144] 40 C.F.R. §§230.5(k) and (l), 230.11, and 230.12(b).

[145] 40 C.F.R. §230.6.

WATER DEPENDENCY

In the short history of the Clean Water Act, a few of the *Guidelines* have been applied more frequently and/or with more sweeping effect than others. One of the more notable *Guidelines* is a regulatory presumption that practicable alternatives which do not involve discharges into wetlands are available when the project "does not require access or proximity to or siting within" a wetland to fulfill the project's basic purpose, i.e., is not "water dependent",[146] unless the applicant can clearly demonstrate otherwise.[147] In other words, if the project is not water-dependent, the Corps must presume that other practicable alternatives are available unless it receives compelling proof to the contrary.

Recently the Corps issued a new Regulatory Guidance Letter which addresses water dependency in the context of cranberry production.[148]

PRACTICABLE ALTERNATIVES

The regulations specifically state that no discharge of dredged or fill material will be permitted if there is a "practicable alternative" to the proposed discharge which

---

[146] Lack of "water-dependency may be very broad. Proposed houses with their own boat slips are not water-dependent. *Korteweg v. U.S. Army Corps of Engineers*, 650 F.Supp. 603 (D.Conn. 1986). On the other hand, a county water supply reservoir was held to be "water-dependent" perhaps on the basis that the "alternatives" proposed by the EPA did not persuade the Court as "practicable". *James City County, Virginia v. EPA*, 955 F.2d 254 (4th Cir. Va. 1992), *cert. denied*, 130 L.Ed.2d 39, 115 S.Ct. 87 (1994).

[147] 40 C.F.R. §230.10(a)(3).

[148] Cranberry production is conceded to be water-dependent. Nonetheless, the activity must be demonstrated to be the least environmentally damaging, including any upland alternative siting. Regulatory Guidance Letter, *Water Dependency and Cranberry Production*, Nº 92-2 (June 26, 1992).

would have less adverse impact on the aquatic ecosystem.[149] Practicable alternatives are presumed to exist for non-water dependent projects unless clearly demonstrated otherwise.[150] "Practicable alternatives" include activities which do not involve a discharge at all or discharges at other locations.[151]

An "alternative" is "practicable" if it is "available and capable of being done after taking into consideration cost, existing technology, and logistics in light of the overall project purposes".[152] Even an area not presently owned by the applicant must be considered.[153] The Corps should accept the applicant's description of the project's purpose,[154] but does not have to accept the applicant's representation that there are no practicable alternatives;[155] it may conduct its own feasibility study of alternative sites and deny a permit if it finds such an alternative site.[156] The applicant is advised to seek the assistance of relevant, experienced professionals in preparing a practicable

---

[149]   40 C.F.R. §230.10(a).

[150]   40 C.F.R. §230.10(a)(3). "Practicable alternatives" are a moving target. For example, depending on the project purpose, unusual standards may apply. See e.g., *Conservation Law Foundation v. FHA*, 827 F.Supp. 871 (D.R.I. 1993), *aff'd.*, 24 F.3d 1465 (1st Cir. P.R. 1994), in which the project purpose of separating through traffic from local traffic militated allowing the filling of wetlands upon a finding of "no practicable alternatives".

[151]   40 C.F.R. §230.10(a)(1).

[152]   40 C.F.R. §230.10(a)(2).

[153]   In *Bersani v. U.S. Environmental Protection Agency, supra.*, the court found that other properties, development of which was less adverse to the environment, were available when the applicant first entered the market to purchase developable land and before it ever applied for a §404 permit. See also *Hough v. Marsh*, 557 F.Supp. 74 (D.Mass. 1982). But see *National Audubon Society v. Hartz Mountain Development Corp.*, 14 Envtl.L.Rep. (Envtl.L.Inst.) 20724 (D.N.J. 1983); *Louisiana Wildlife Federation, Inc. v. York*, 603 F.Supp. 518 (W.D.La.), *aff'd in part and vacated in part*, 761 F.2d 1044 (5th Cir. 1985); *Sylvester v. U.S. Army Corps of Engineers*, 882 F.2d 407 (9th Cir. Cal. 1989).

[154]   *Louisiana Wildlife Federation, Inc. v. York*, 761 F.2d 1044 (5th Cir. La. 1985).

[155]   *Shoreline Assocs. v. Marsh, supra.* See also *James City County v. EPA, supra.*

[156]   *Deltona Corporation v. Alexander*, 504 F.Supp. 1280 (M.D.Fla. 1981), *aff'd.*, 682 F.2d 888 (11th Cir. Fla. 1982).

alternatives study for presentation to the Corps along with the permit application.

SIGNIFICANT DEGRADATION OF WATER

Similar to the "recapture provision" applicable to Nationwide Permits, the regulations provide that even if the applicant can pass all of the factual determinations and minimization requirements, if the Corps still finds that the project's discharge would cause a "significant degradation of waters of the United States", the Corps may deny a permit.[157] The finding of a significant degradation must be based upon the factual determinations, evaluations, and tests described above but it must also pay special heed to the "persistence and permanence" of the adverse effects and may be considered individually or collectively.[158]

Some of these catch-all adverse effects are the discharge of pollutants which affects human health or welfare (including municipal water supplies, plankton, fish, shellfish, wildlife, and special aquatic sites); on the life stages of aquatic life and other wildlife dependent on aquatic ecosystems (including the transfer, concentration, and spread of pollutants or their by products outside of the disposal site through biological, physical, and chemical processes); on aquatic ecosystem diversity, productivity, and stability (including loss of fish and wildlife habitat or the loss of the capacity of a wetland to assimilate nutrients, purify water, or reduce wave energy); and, on recreational, aesthetic, and economic values.

---

[157]   40 C.F.R. §230.10(c).

[158]   *Id.*

OTHER CONSIDERATIONS

Non-Wetlands Environmental Effects

The Corps may consider other factors than simply the direct effect of a discharge of dredged or fill material in a wetland when making its permit decision. As has been discussed above, there are many opportunities in the regulations for the Corps to accept advice and comments from other agencies particularly the U.S. Fish and Wildlife Service.[159] State and local land use and zoning decisions will not be considered.[160]

Socio-Economic Effects

The Corps is permitted to consider to a limited extent socio-economic effects of permit applications under §10 of the Rivers and Harbors Act but not under §404 of the Clean Water Act.[161] However, the Corps insists that it will continue to consider socio-economic effects although district engineers are cautioned to "give less weight to impacts that are, at best, weakly related to the purpose of our permit action and statutory authority, and not let such impacts be the sole or most important basis for a permit denial".[162]

Indirect Effects

The Corps has attempted to distinguish between attenuated and non-attenuated indirect impacts and tries to consider the attenuated indirect impacts less heavily. Some

---

[159] 33 C.F.R. §320.4.

[160] 33 C.F.R. §320.4(j)(2).

[161] *Mall Properties, Inc. v. Marsh, supra.*

[162] Regulatory Guidance Letter, *Mall Properties, Inc. v. Marsh*, № 88-11 (August 22, 1988), ¶4.

examples of indirect impacts are water withdrawals for hydroelectric power generation on downstream aquatic communities and spin-off development from a major project. The Corps considers the spin-off development to be attenuated and thus not entitled to "heavy" consideration. On the other hand, the effect on downstream aquatic communities, while also indirect, is not attenuated and thus must be considered "heavily".[163]

Mitigation

Mitigation is the subject of sometimes passionate disagreement, both between the Corps and the Environmental Protection Agency and between environmentalists and the regulated community. Repairing the damaged functions of an existing wetland presents one set of arguments over the effectiveness of such an effort over time. The concept of building a new wetland where none existed before draws even more loud voices pro and con over whether such a creation will ever be operative at all. Add to these disagreements the doubts whether there is a scientific method sufficient to accomplish mimicry of nature, the sometimes massive expense of the undertaking, and one returns to the root question, "Why did an existing wetland get damaged or destroyed at all?".

Mitigation differs from the previously-discussed "minimization" in the permit-issuing regulations. "Minimization" requires that the impacts of the proposed activity on a wetland be held to a minimum from the outset of the project design.[164] "Mitigation" comes into play only after the amount of wetland damage has been reduced to its barest minimum but there will still be some damage which must be mitigated.

---

[163] *Id., Riverside Irrigation District v. Andrews*, 758 F.2d 508 (10th Cir. 1985).

[164] 33 C.F.R. §320.4(r).

Effective February 7, 1990, the Corps and the Environmental Protection Agency entered into a *Memorandum Of Agreement Between the U.S. Environmental Protection Agency and U.S. Department of the Army Concerning the Determination of Mitigation Under The Clean Water Act Section 404(b)(1) Guidelines*, (February 7, 1990) (hereinafter the *Mitigation MOA*). This *Mitigation MOA* contains a detailed exposition of the mandatory sequence of analysis when considering applications for individual permits which involve issues of compliance with the *Guidelines*. The *Mitigation MOA* recognizes that the national goal of no net loss of wetlands functions and values may not be achieved in every individual permit action because individual mitigation measures are "not feasible, not practicable, or would accomplish only inconsequential reductions in impacts".[165]

In considering whether to allow mitigation, the Corps is required to follow a specific sequence: first it must determine that potential impacts have been avoided to the maximum extent possible, then it must determine that remaining unavoidable impacts will be mitigated "to the extent appropriate and practicable by requiring steps to minimize impacts, and then to compensate for aquatic resource values.[166] The Corps may "deviate" from this sequence when the Corps and the Environmental Protection Agency "agree that the proposed discharge is necessary to avoid environmental harm (e.g., to protect a natural aquatic community from saltwater intrusion, chemical contamination, or other deleterious physical or chemical impacts), or the Environmental Protection Agency and the Corps agree that the proposed discharge can reasonably be expected to result in environmental gain or insignificant environmental losses".[167] Further, the *Mitigation MOA* allows a flexible determination of "appropriate and practicable", i.e., one which is "appropriate to the scope and degree of those impacts and practicable in terms of cost, existing technology, and logistics in light of overall

---

[165] *Mitigation MOA*, ¶B.

[166] *Mitigation MOA*, ¶C.

[167] *Mitigation MOA*, ¶C.

project purposes".[168]

The overriding principle of permit issuance is the avoidance of impacts such that no discharge will be permitted if there is a practicable alternative to the proposed discharge which would have a less adverse impact on the aquatic ecosystem, so long as the alternative does not have other significant adverse environmental consequences.[169] Therefore, the first step for the Corps is to determine the least environmentally damaging practicable alternative. Compensatory mitigation is forbidden in this early determination as a method to reduce environmental impacts.

The second step is for the Corps to require appropriate and practicable project modifications and permit conditions in order to minimize the adverse impacts. The *Mitigation MOA* refers the Corps to Subpart H of the *Guidelines* (40 C.F.R. §§230.70-230.77) for the means of minimizing impacts.

Finally, appropriate and practicable compensatory mitigation is required for those impacts remaining after the foregoing avoidance and minimization steps have been satisfied, for the so called "unavoidable" impacts. Compensatory mitigation contemplates the restoration of existing degraded wetlands or the creation of man-made wetlands first of all on-site, or in areas adjacent or contiguous to the discharge site, and only secondarily off-site in the same geographic area (defined as close physical proximity and, to the extent possible, the same watershed) if practicable. In addition to the preference for on-site compensatory mitigation over off-site, the Corps must consider the functional values lost by the resource impacted with particular attention to be paid to the likelihood of success of the effort. Since wetland creation is an uncertain endeavor, restoration is the preferred method of compensatory mitigation.

The *Mitigation MOA* mentions a concept called "mitigation banking". Under this new concept, existing wetlands may be purchased and used as compensatory mitigation only if the Corps and the Environmental Protection Agency approve the use of the bank

---

[168] *Id.*

[169] *Mitigation MOA*, ¶C.1, citing 40 C.F.R. §230.10(a).

for specified identified projects regardless of the practicability of other forms of compensatory mitigation. The Environmental Protection Agency has developed further specific guidance on this subject.[170]

In considering the amount of required compensatory mitigation in the case of unavoidably impacted wetlands, the *Mitigation MOA* requires a one-to-one acreage replacement of functions and values as a "reasonable surrogate" with "an adequate margin of safety to reflect the expected degree of success associated with the mitigation plan, recognizing that this minimum requirement may not be appropriate and practicable, and thus may not be relevant in all cases".[171] The one-to-one requirement may be modified if the functional values of the impacted wetland are high and the likelihood of success of the mitigation project is low, or, inversely, if the functional value is low and the likelihood of success is high.

The *Mitigation MOA* also requires that mitigators engage in monitoring the compensatory mitigation especially in areas of "scientific uncertainty".[172] If the Corps determines that the mitigation effort is failing, it is authorized to follow the procedures outlined for enforcement in 33 C.F.R. §326 to "ensure those waters (of the United States) are not misused and to maintain the integrity of the program".[173] A permissible permit condition is to require long-term monitoring in mitigation efforts involving "higher levels of scientific uncertainty",[174] however, if the mitigation plan is neither

---

[170]   On December 20, 1991, Region IX of the Environmental Protection Agency (San Francisco) issued a *Mitigation Banking Guidance*. In addition, on March 6, 1995, the Corps, Environmental Protection Agency, Natural Resources Conservation Service of the Department of Agriculture, the Fish and Wildlife Service of the Department of the Interior, and the National Oceanic and Atmospheric Administration of the Department of Commerce issued a proposed *Federal Guidance for the Establishment, Use and Operation of Mitigation Banks*. 60 Fed.Reg. 43, pp. 12286-12293.

[171]   *Mitigation MOA*, ¶III.B.

[172]   *Mitigation MOA*, ¶III.D.

[173]   33 C.F.R. §326.2, "Policy".

[174]   *Mitigation MOA*, ¶III.D and ¶III.E.

"reasonably implementable or enforceable, the permit shall be denied".[175]

Other Approvals

In addition to obtaining a §404 permit, applicants must always obtain a state water quality certificate, and frequently must obtain other approvals as well.[176] In fact, the Corps will cease processing a permit without these approvals but can process a §404 permit concurrently with the processing of these other approvals.[177] The Corps, too, is required to consult with other agencies with respect to permit review.[178]

State Water Quality Certification

The Clean Water Act and the regulations require that any applicant for a §404 permit "that may result in a discharge of a pollutant into waters of the United States" also obtain a certification from the discharge-originating state or the interstate water pollution control agency which has jurisdiction over the point source of the pollution that the discharge will comply with the "applicable effluent limitations and water quality standards".[179] Although technically no permit will be granted until the

---

[175] *Mitigation MOA*, ¶III.E.

[176] Regulatory Guidance Letter, *Regulatory Thresholds*, Nº 88-12 (September 9, 1988).

[177] 33 C.F.R. §320.4(j)(1).

[178] 33 U.S.C. §1344(q); *Memorandum of Agreement Between the Environmental Protection Agency and the Department of the Army Concerning Clean Water Act Section 404(q)*, (August 11, 1992); *Memorandum of Agreement Between the Department of Commerce and the Department of the Army Concerning Clean Water Act Section 404(q)*, (August 11, 1992); *Memorandum of Agreement between the Department of the Interior and the Department of the Army, Concerning Clean water Act Section 404(q)*, (December 21, 1992). If there is a dispute between the Corps and these agencies, these *Memoranda* require that the dispute be "elevated" to a higher level within the agency so as to avoid delay in individual permit decisions when there is policy dispute.

[179] 33 U.S.C. §1341; 33 C.F.R. §§320.3(a), 320.4(d), and 325(b)(1). State certification of water

(continued...)

certification has been obtained, a waiver by the certifying agency may be deemed to have occurred if the agency fails to act within sixty days of the request.[180] The Corps has the authority to notify the agency that a shorter period of time than sixty days may be required, and, conversely, the Corps may determine that a longer period will be necessary based on information provided by the agency.[181] In no event will this time enlargement last longer than one year.[182]

Once the certification has been issued prior to the permit decision, any subsequent denial or modification of the certification will not affect ordinarily a §404 permit but the Corps may consider the subsequent denial or modification as part of the public interest review and may respond accordingly.[183] However, if the Corps finds that there has been a "sufficient change" in the project such then the Corps may require that a new water quality certification be applied for.[184] An exception to this process is when a state court voids a certification prior to the §404 permit issuance.[185] In that case, the Corps cannot issue the §404 permit until the certification is "legally revived", i.e., by the appellate process, re-issuance, or waiver.[186]

After the §404 permit has been issued, a subsequent denial or modification of

---

[179](...continued)
quality will be conclusive evidence of compliance unless the Environmental Protection Agency intervenes. Regulatory Guidance Letter, *Water Quality Considerations*, Nº 90-4 (March 13, 1990).

[180] 33 C.F.R. §325.2(b)(1)(ii).

[181] *Id*.

[182] *Id*.

[183] Regulatory Guidance Letter, *Section 401 Water Quality Certification*, Nº 87-3, ¶2.b.

[184] *Id*.

[185] There is no review of state water quality certificates in federal court. *Roosevelt Campobello International Park Commission v. U.S. Environmental Protection Agency*, 684 F.2d 1041 (1st Cir. 1982).

[186] Regulatory Guidance Letter, *Water Quality Consideration*, Nº 90-4 (March 13, 1990).

a certification or the certification is voided by a court, will not necessarily affect the terms of the §404 permit but the Corps may consider modification, suspension, or revocation of the §404 permit.

Coastal Zone Management Program

Obviously not all states have a coastal zone management program but among those that do, the Coastal Zone Management Act, 16 U.S.C. §1456(c), requires the applicant to furnish another certification that the proposed activity will comply with the state's coastal zone management program.[187] The procedure for obtaining the certificate is a little different from the water quality certification. The applicant submits his "certification" directly to the Corps which then sends a copy of the public notice, including the applicant's certification, to the National Oceanic and Atmospheric Administration (which administers the federal Coastal Zone Management Act,[188] and to the relevant state coastal zone management agency requesting its concurrence or objection.[189] If the state agency objects, the Corps cannot issue the §404 permit until the state agency concurs or is overruled by the Secretary of Commerce on the grounds that the proposed activity is consistent with the federal coastal zone management program or is "necessary in the interest of national security".[190] The state agency has only six months to concur or object after which concurrence is conclusively presumed.

---

[187]   33 C.F.R. §320.3(b).

[188]   16 U.S.C. §§1451, *et seq.*; 33 C.F.R. §§320.3(b) and 320.4(h).

[189]   33 C.F.R. §325.2(b)(2)(ii). The individual state may require a separate permit. Furthermore, the states may limit application of a Nationwide Permit in a coastal zone. See Regulatory Guidance Letter, *Section 401 Water Quality Certification and Coastal Zone Management Act Conditions for Nationwide Permits*, Nº 92-4 (September 14, 1992). If a state has developed a Special Area Management Plan, another Regulatory Guidance Letter, Nº 92-3, extends the expiration of Regulatory Guidance Letter 86-10 with respect to these areas.

[190]   *Id.*

Marine Protection, Research, and Sanctuaries Act

The applicant should determine whether his proposed activities will take place in an area which has been designated as a marine sanctuary by the Secretary of Commerce under the Marine Protection, Research, and Sanctuaries Act, 16 U.S.C. §1432.[191] If so, then the proposed activities must also be certified by the Secretary as consistent with the purposes of the Act and consistent with the regulations under the Act. Generally these areas are in coastal areas.

Environmental Impact Statement

The regulations require that the provisions of the National Environmental Policy Act apply to the §404 permit process although generally only for small portions of larger federal projects.[192] For most §404 permit applications, the Corps will require only an Environmental Assessment, reserving the requirement of a full Environmental Impact Statement for large projects with considerable federal involvement.

National Historic Preservation Act

Under the National Historic Preservation Act, the Advisory Council on Historic Preservation is authorized to review and comment upon federally-licensed activities which will have an effect upon properties listed (or eligible for listing) in the National Register of Historic Places.[193] Whenever a project "alters any terrain such that significant historical or archaeological data is threatened, the Secretary of the Interior may take action necessary to recover and preserve the data prior to the commencement

---

[191]   33 C.F.R. §320.3(c).

[192]   33 C.F.R. §320.3(d).

[193]   16 U.S.C. §470; 33 C.F.R. §§320.3(g) and 325.2(b)(3); 36 C.F.R §800.

of the project".[194] The Corps's regulations state that §404 permit application actions "should, insofar as possible, be consistent with, and avoid significant adverse effects on the values or purposes for which" a classification such as the National Register of Historic Places was established.[195] The Corps should attempt to reach an agreement with the Federal Advisory Council on Historic Preservation on how the project will be carried out but, if no agreement is possible, the Corps may proceed to permit issuance without it.[196]

Interstate Land Sales Full Disclosure Act

The Interstate Land Sales Full Disclosure Act (15 U.S.C. §1701 *et seq.*) requires a developer, prior to selling or leasing any lot in a subdivision (defined in 15 U.S.C. §1701(3)), to provide a written report which states whether or not a §404 permit has been applied for, issued, or denied; and/or whether any enforcement action has been taken as a consequence of any non-application for or denial of a permit.[197]

Endangered Species Act

The Endangered Species Act declares a dual intent to conserve threatened and endangered species as well as the ecosystems on which those species depend.[198] In conserving ecosystems, even those beyond the geographic area of the project in question if the Corps finds that the activity will have a physical effect on off-site endangered species or if the project can be redesigned to avoid the effect on

---

[194]   33 C.F.R. §320.3(g).

[195]   33 C.F.R. §320.4(e). See also Appendix C to 33 C.F.R. §§325.

[196]   36 C.F.R. §800.5.

[197]   33 C.F.R. §320.3(h).

[198]   16 U.S.C. §§1531 *et seq.*

endangered species,[199] the Corps must consult with the U.S. Fish and Wildlife Service and the National Marine Fisheries Service to take any action necessary to insure that a §404 licensed project "is not likely to jeopardize the continued existence of such endangered or threatened species or result in the destruction or adverse modification of habitat of such species" which the Secretaries of Commerce or Interior have determined to be critical.[200]

Environmental Protection Agency Veto Authority

Section 404© of the Clean Water Act authorizes the Environmental Protection Agency to veto the issuance of a permit if it determines, "after notice and opportunity for public hearings, that the discharge . . . will have an unacceptable adverse effect on municipal water supplies, shellfish beds, and fishery areas (including spawning and breeding areas), wildlife, or recreational areas".[201] Thus, notwithstanding any of the foregoing, and although it has done so only very rarely, the Environmental Protection Agency can veto a permit issuance even though the proposed activities are within all of the *Guidelines* and other statutory authorities and regulations.

---

[199] *Riverside Irrigation District v. Andrews*, 758 F.2d 508 (10th Cir. 1985); *Winnebago Tribe of Nebraska v. Ray*, 621 F.2d 269 (8th Cir. 1980), *cert. denied*, 449 U.S. 836, 66 L.Ed.2d 43, 101 S.Ct. 110 (1980); *Save the Bay, Inc. v. U.S. Army Corps of Engineers*, 610 F.2d 322 (5th Cir. 1980), *cert. denied*, 449 U.S. 900, 66 L.Ed.2d 130, 101 S.Ct. 269 (1980).

[200] 33 C.F.R. §320.3(I).

[201] 33 U.S.C. §1344(c).

CHAPTER SEVEN
ADMINISTRATIVE PENALTIES

The power to penalize the discharge of dredged or fill material into a wetland without a permit, or a violation of a condition of an existing permit, stems from two statutory sources: the Environmental Protection Agency's power to issue administrative orders for unpermitted fills under §309(a)(3),[202] and the Corps's power to issue "cease and desist" orders in the form of letters to permit violators under §404(s).[203]

---

[202] "Whenever on the basis of any information available to him the Administrator (of the Environmental Protection Agency) finds that any person is in violation of section 1311 (which makes the discharge of pollutants illegal except in compliance with the law), 1312 (establishing water quality related effluent limitations), 1316 (establishing standards of performance for the control of the discharge of pollutants), 1317 (establishing toxic and pretreatment effluent standards), 1318 (requiring owners and operators of point sources to keep records of effluents data, report such data, and allow entry to his or her premises and records), 1328 (allowing the discharge of specific pollutants under controlled conditions associated with an approved aquaculture project), or 1345 (governing the issuance of permits for the disposal of sewage sludge) of this title, or is in violation of any permit condition or limitation implementing any of such sections in a permit issued under section 1342 of this title by him or by a State or in a permit issued under section 1344 of this title by a State, he shall issue an order requiring such person to comply with such section or requirement, or he shall bring a civil action in accordance with subsection (b) of this section." 33 U.S.C. §1319(a)(3).

"The Administrator is authorized to commence a civil action or appropriate relief, including a permanent or temporary injunction, for any violation for which he is authorized to issue a compliance order under subsection (a) of this section. Any action under this subsection may be brought in the district court of the United States for the district in which the defendant is located or resides or is doing business, and such court shall have jurisdiction to restrain such violation and to require compliance. Notice of the commencement of such action shall be given immediately to the appropriate State." 33 U.S.C. §1319(b).

[203] "(1) Whenever on the basis of any information available to him the Secretary (of the Army) finds that any person is in violation of any condition or limitation set forth in a permit issued by the Secretary under this section, the Secretary shall issue an order requiring such person to comply with such condition or limitation, or the Secretary shall bring a civil action in accordance with paragraph (3) of this subsection.

(2) A copy of any order issued under this subsection shall be sent immediately by the

(continued...)

ENVIRONMENTAL PROTECTION AGENCY PENALTIES

In addition to issuing administrative orders, the Environmental Protection Agency can assess two kinds of administrative penalties, called "Class I" for lesser violations, and "Class II" for serious violations[204], which will take the form of an

---

(continued...)
Secretary to the State in which the violation occurs and other affected States. Any order issued under this subsection shall be by personal service and shall state with reasonable specificity the nature of the violation, specify a time for compliance, not to exceed thirty days, which the Secretary determines is reasonable, taking into account the seriousness of the violation and any good faith efforts to comply with applicable requirements. In any case in which an order under this subsection is issued to a corporation, a copy of such order shall be served on any appropriate corporate officers.

(3) The Secretary is authorized to commence a civil action for appropriate relief, including a permanent or temporary injunction for any violation for which he is authorized to issue a compliance order under paragraph (1) of this subsection. Any action under this paragraph may be brought in the district court of the United States for the district in which the defendant is located or resides or is doing business, and such court shall have jurisdiction to restrain such violation and to require compliance. Notice of the commencement of such action shall be given immediately to the appropriate State.

(4) Any person who violates any condition or limitation in a permit issued by the Secretary under this section, and any person who violates any order issued by the Secretary under paragraph (1) of this subsection, shall be subject to a civil penalty not to exceed $25,000 per day for each violation. In determining the amount of a civil penalty the court shall consider the seriousness of the violation or violations, the economic benefit (if any) resulting from the violation, any history of such violations, any good faith efforts to comply with applicable requirements, the economic impact of the penalty on the violator, and such other matters as justice may require. 33 U.S.C. §1344(s).

[204] "(2) Classes of penalties
(A) Class I
The amount of a class I civil penalty under paragraph 1 may not exceed $10,000 per violation, except that the maximum amount of any class I civil penalty under this subparagraph shall not exceed $25,000. Before issuing an order assessing a civil penalty under this subparagraph, the Administrator or the Secretary, as the case may be, shall give to the person assessed such penalty written notice of the Administrator's or Secretary's proposal to issue such order and the opportunity to request, within 30 days of the date the notice is received by such person, a hearing on the proposed order. Such hearing shall not be subject to section 554 or 556 (of the federal Administrative Procedure Act requiring a trial-like hearing before a hearing officer), but shall provide a reasonable opportunity to be heard and to present evidence.
(B) Class II
The amount of a class II civil penalty under paragraph (1) may not exceed $10,000 per day for each day during which the violation continues; except that the maximum amount of any class II civil penalty under this subparagraph shall not exceed $125,000. Except as otherwise provided in this

(continued...)

114

administrative complaint, including a calculation of the amount of the administrative penalty.[205] The Environmental Protection Agency has developed a *Clean Water Act Section 404 Civil Administrative Penalty Actions: Guidance On Calculating Settlement Amounts*[206] for Class I and Class II violations, in which six factors are listed which will be considered in determining the amount of the initial demand:

(1) the nature, circumstances, extent, and gravity of the violation (including an assessment of the environmental impacts of the violation, the significance of the resource(s), general national environmental goals, and professional experience);

(2) the economic benefit to the violator (in order to remove any economic benefit from the violator's failure to comply);

(3) the violator's ability to pay (but only if the violator raises this issue and provides appropriately certified documentation of his or her financial condition);

(4) prior violations of the Clean Water Act (which may be obtained from the Corps or any other federal agency);

(5) the violator's degree of culpability (including the violator's

---

subsection, a class II civil penalty shall be assessed and collected in the same manner, and subject to the same provisions, as in the case of civil penalties assessed and collected after notice and opportunity for a hearing on the record in accordance with section 554 (of the federal Administrative Procedure Act). The Administrator and the Secretary may issue rules for discovery procedures for hearings under this subparagraph." 33 U.S.C. §1319(g)(2). See also 40 C.F.R. §22(a)(6).

[205]   40 C.F.R. §22.14(a)(4).

[206]   Hereinafter the "Penalty Calculation Guidance". This Penalty Calculation Guidance is dated December 14, 1990.

previous experience with §404 permitting requirements and the degree of control the violator had over the illegal conduct); and

(6)   other factors that justice may require (including mitigating, such as the amount of any state-imposed penalty) as well as aggravating, such as the violator's lack of cooperation, circumstances.

Under the Penalty Calculation Guidance, the Environmental Protection Agency will first calculate the "economic benefit of noncompliance". The "economic benefit of noncompliance" is defined in the Penalty Calculation Guidance as including the increased property value directly resulting from the violation, unless an after-the-fact permit has been issued, in which case the increased property value would not include the permanent increased property value, but may include the violator's temporary profits realized prior to issuance of the after-the-fact permit. Economic benefit may also be adjusted upward to include the violator's delayed costs of removal or restoration whether or not an after-the-fact permit is issued, and the violator's avoided costs of, for example, properly disposing of the fill material in an upland site vs. discharging it into a wetland. Another element of economic benefit includes the profit accrued by the violator which he or she would not have accrued but for the illegal discharge, such as profits from agriculture, commercial hunting, logging, or aquaculture made before the violator ceased operation, removed the discharge, restored the property, or before the after-the-fact permit was issued. Economic benefit may also include the profits realized by a violator who is not the owner of the property, e.g., the contractor who actually committed the violation. The Penalty Calculation Guidance urges the "case development team" to use its "best professional judgment" to identify the types of economic benefit (of which there may be several—and all of which must be included in the total amount), to identify the information needed to make the calculation, and to determine the most appropriate method for obtaining the information needed.

Next the Environmental Protection Agency will calculate the "environmental significance" of the violation. "Environmental significance" is deliberately loosely defined as it is "appropriately evaluated over a range of impacts" and will "depend on a variety of factors unique to the circumstances of each case". Some criteria are:

(1) the significance of the impact under the *Guidelines*;

(2) the acreage of the aquatic area affected;

(3) the duration of the illegal discharge;

(4) the chemical nature of the discharged material; and

(5) the pre-existing quality of the aquatic site.

The Environmental Protection Agency recognizes, however, that the loss of a small-but-high-quality wetland may draw a higher penalty than the loss of large-but-low-quality wetland after consideration of such factors as functions and values performed (see Chapter 2, above), location, and the cumulative losses within that system of the violation and the "compliance significance" of the violator using a "Section 404 Penalty Matrix".

Under the Section 404 Penalty Matrix, if the compliance significance is "minor" (considering the violator's degree of culpability, his or her history of compliance vs. any previous violations, and the deterrence value of the case either against the individual violator or others in the regulated community), and the environmental significance is also "minor" (where a discharge which impacts a low-quality wetland, or has negligible impacts on moderate- or high-quality wetlands), the penalty will range from $500 to $5,000. If the environmental significance is "moderate" (those in which a discharge jeopardizes the functions and values of a wetland which is neither low- or high-quality, which performs relatively few ecological functions, or where cumulative losses have been few), the penalty will range from $5,001 to $15,000. If the environmental significance is "major" (a discharge which causes, individually or cumulatively, directly or indirectly, significant environmental effects to high-quality wetlands, causes or contributes to violations of state water quality standards, violates a toxic effluent standard or prohibition, jeopardizes the continued existence of endangered or threatened species, will result in the likely destruction or adverse modification of designated critical habitat under state or federal law, or causes or contributes to significant degradation to wetlands, i.e., has an effect on municipal water supplies, on the life stages of aquatic life or other wildlife dependent on the wetland ecosystem, on ecosystem diversity, productivity, and stability, and on recreation or aesthetic values), the penalty will range from $15,001 to $40,000.

If the compliance significance is "moderate" (in which, for example, the violator has less than full responsibility or shares responsibility with others) but the environmental significance is minor, the penalty will range from $5,001 to $15,000. If the environmental significance is "moderate", the penalty will range from $15,001 to $40,000. If the environmental significance is "major, the penalty will range from $40,001 to $75,000.

If the compliance significance is "major" (when the violator knew or should have known of the need to obtain a permit for the activity, or has one or more previous violations on his or her record, which may cause a judicial referral instead of an administrative penalty) but the environmental significance is minor, the penalty will range from $15,001 to $40,000. If the environmental significance is "moderate", the penalty will range from $40,001 to $75,000. If the environmental significance is "major", the penalty will range from $75,001 to $125,000.

The final step in making the calculation of the penalty is the Environmental Protection Agency's consideration of "relevant adjustment factors", such as the violator's recalcitrance (e.g. failure to cooperate by providing information, to cease activity, to allow access to the property, or to remove the fill or restore the wetland), his or her ability to pay (which may require evaluation by an outside financial consultant if the issue is raised by the violator and the violator sustains his or her burden of establishing inability to pay), and "litigation considerations" (including case law, competing public interest considerations, or specific facts or evidentiary issues pertaining to the individual case). Having determined these numbers, the Environmental Protection Agency will then determine the appropriate amount of the penalty by adding together the economic benefit component and the environmental and compliance significance component, and modify the total by the adjustment factors to arrive at a final dollar amount for the penalty, which will be included in the administrative complaint.

Class I Violations

Alleged violators who wish to contest the administrative penalty assessed by the Environmental Protection Agency may appeal the issuance of the penalty. In the case of a Class I penalty, the alleged violator may request a hearing within thirty days of receipt of the notice of the penalty.[207] Class I hearings are relatively informal but there must be at least an opportunity to present evidence.[208] If still not satisfied with the result, the next level of appeal, which must also be filed within thirty days of the date the penalty order is issued, is to the United States District Court for the District of Columbia or in the district in which the violation occurred.[209] A copy of the notice of appeal must also be sent by certified mail to the Administrator, if the Environmental Protection Agency is assessing the penalty, or to the Secretary of the Army, if the Corps is assessing the penalty.[210] The Administrator shall "promptly" file a certified copy of

---

[207]   33 U.S.C. §1319(g)(2).

[208]   33 U.S.C. §1319(g)(2)(A).

[209]   33 U.S.C. §1319(g)(8)(A).

[210]   *Id.* See also "Corps Penalties", below.

the record on which the penalty order was issued with the appropriate court. These appeals are difficult for the alleged violator to win as the Clean Water Act expressly states that "[s]uch court shall not set aside or remand such order unless there is *not substantial evidence* in the record, taken as a whole, to support the finding of a violation or unless the Administrator's or Secretary's assessment of the penalty constitutes an abuse of discretion. . . ".[211] The court cannot impose any additional penalties for the same violation unless the Administrator's or Secretary's assessment constitutes an abuse of discretion.[212]

Class II Violations

In the case of a Class II penalty, violators are entitled to a full, adjudicatory hearing following rules set forth in the federal Administrative Procedure Act and the Environmental Protection Agency's regulations.[213] An alleged violator has twenty days to answer the administrative complaint and request a hearing.[214] If he or she does not answer, once the Environmental Protection Agency has made out a *prima facie* case, a default may be entered sixty days after service of the complaint, whereupon the assessed penalty becomes immediately payable without any further proceeding.[215]

Assuming that the violator requested a hearing, there are regulations governing the conduct of the hearing,[216] at the end of which the hearing officer will issue an

---

[211]   *Id*. (emphasis added).

[212]   *Id*. Logically this could only occur if the abuse of discretion found by the court is that the penalty amount was ridiculously low.

[213]   33 U.S.C.§1319(g)(2)(B); 5 U.S.C. §554; 40 C.F.R. §22.

[214]   40 C.F.R. §22.15(a).

[215]   40 C.F.R. §22.17(a).

[216]   40 C.F.R. §§22.21 through 22.26.

"initial decision".[217] A motion to reopen the hearing to present additional evidence may be filed within twenty days of the issuance of the initial decision.[218] There may be interlocutory appeals brought before the hearing has concluded, and there may be an appeal of the initial decision directly to the Environmental Protection Agency Administrator within twenty days of the initial decision.[219] Intervention is permitted in this appellate process as well as *amicus curiae* participation.[220]

A violator may also seek judicial review of a Class II penalty in the United States Court of Appeals for the District of Columbia Circuit, or any other federal circuit court of appeals in which the violator resides or does business so long as the appeal is brought within thirty days of final issuance of the penalty order.[221]

CORPS PENALTIES

The Corps also has authority to issue administrative penalties for permit violations (as opposed to the Environmental Protection Agency's authority over unpermitted discharges) although they are different in amount and procedure from the Environmental Protection Agency's penalty regulations. The Corps can assess penalties of up to $10,000 for each permit violation up to a total maximum penalty of $25,000.[222] Corps penalty proceedings are initiated by the District Engineer preparing and processing a proposed order, specifying the amount of the penalty and stating with

---

[217] 40 C.F.R. §22.27.

[218] 40 C.F.R. §22.30.

[219] 40 C.F.R. §§22.29(a), 22.29(b), 22.30.

[220] 40 C.F.R. §§22.11 and 22.30(a)(2).

[221] 33 U.S.C. §1319(g)(8)(B).

[222] 33 C.F.R. §326.6(a)(1).

reasonable specificity the nature of the violation.[223] The proposed order is to be served on the permittee giving him or her thirty days to request a hearing.[224] The district engineer must also give public notice of the proposed order, provide a reasonable opportunity for public comment on the proposed order,[225] and notify the appropriate state agency of the proposed order.[226] If the permittee does not request a hearing, those members of the public who submitted written comments will be given notice of the final order and have thirty days to petition to have the order set aside and provide a hearing.[227] The District Engineer does not have to hold a hearing if the evidence presented by the public commentator is either immaterial or was already considered when the order was issued.[228]

The permittee must specify in his or her written request for a hearing a summary of the factual and legal issues in dispute and the legal grounds for the permittee's defense.[229] The hearing must be scheduled "promptly" but not before the 30-day public comment period has expired.[230] The hearing must be a "fair and impartial proceeding in which the participants (the permittee, those members of the public who submitted written comments, and anyone attending the hearing) are given a reasonable opportunity to present evidence.[231] Other Corps regulations specify the rules for

---

[223]   33 C.F.R. §326.6(b)(1).

[224]   33 C.F.R. §§326.6(b)(2) and 326.6(g)(1).

[225]   33 C.F.R. §§326.6(b)(3) and 326.6(c).

[226]   33 C.F.R. §§326.6(b)(4) and 326.6(d).

[227]   33 C.F.R. §326.6(c)(3).

[228]   *Id.*

[229]   33 C.F.R. §326.6(g)(1).

[230]   33 C.F.R. §326.6(g)(3).

[231]   33 C.F.R. §326.6(h).

conducting the hearing itself and for issuance of a final order.[232] Final orders become effective 30 days after issuance unless an appeal is taken.[233] There is no administrative review of final orders but judicial review is available by filing a notice of appeal in the United States District Court for either the District of Columbia or in the district in which the permit violation was alleged to have occurred within thirty days of issuance of the final order.[234] The notice of appeal must also be sent by certified mail to the District Engineer and the Attorney General.[235]

FAILURE TO PAY

Failure to pay the penalty after all appeals have failed allows the Administrator or Secretary to request the Attorney General to bring a civil action to recover the amount assessed.[236] The validity, amount, and appropriateness of the penalty may not be re-litigated in this proceeding but there may be a motion to reconsider filed within 10 days after service of the final order.[237] In addition to the penalty, the Attorney General is also required to ask for interest, attorneys fees, and costs for the collection proceeding, as well as a "quarterly nonpayment penalty" equal to 20% of the aggregate of the original penalty plus any other unpaid nonpayment penalties which are unpaid as of the beginning of the quarter in which the proceedings commenced.[238]

---

[232]   33 C.F.R. §§326.6(I) and (j).

[233]   33 C.F.R. §326.6(k).

[234]   33 C.F.R. §326.6(l).

[235]   33 C.F.R. §326.6(l)(3).

[236]   33 U.S.C. §1319(g)(9); 40 C.F.R. §22.31(b).

[237]   40 C.F.R. §22.31(b).

[238]   33 U.S.C. §1319(g)(9).

CHAPTER EIGHT
ENFORCEMENT PROCEDURES

GOVERNMENT INVESTIGATION

As a practical matter, because the Corps has more field personnel, it will conduct the initial investigation.[239] However, the Enforcement MOA establishes a concept called the "lead enforcement agency" and proceeds to allocate responsibility between the Corps and Environmental Protection Agency depending upon the type of violation.[240] In the case of simple unpermitted discharges, the Corps is the lead enforcement agency subject to four exceptions:

(1)   if the unpermitted activity involves repeat violator(s);

(2)   if the violation is "flagrant";

(3)   if the Environmental Protection Agency requests a class of cases or a particular case; or

(4)   if the Corps recommends that an Environmental Protection Agency administrative penalty may be warranted.[241]

---

[239] *Memorandum of Agreement Between The Department of the Army and the Environmental Protection Agency Concerning Federal Enforcement for the Section 404 Program of the Clean Water Act,* ¶II.A (January 19, 1989) (hereinafter the "Enforcement MOA").

[240] Enforcement MOA, ¶II.D and ¶III.D.

[241] Enforcement MOA, ¶III.D.1.

The Corps is the lead enforcement agency in (1) cases involving permit condition violations; (2) cases in which the Environmental Protection Agency has notified the Corps that it will not take the case; and (3) if the Environmental Protection Agency asks the Corps to take action on a permit condition violation.[242] In any of these possible lead enforcement selections, if the Corps determines that there is not violation of a permit condition, that is the end of the inquiry for the governmental enforcement.[243]

Although the Corps and the Environmental Protection Agency are the only two authorized enforcement agencies,[244] the Enforcement MOA requires them to seek and accept assistance from the U.S. Fish and Wildlife Service, the National Marine Fisheries Service, and any other federal, state, tribal, or local agency "when appropriate".[245] Obviously the U.S. Fish and Wildlife Service is in the best position to detect and report violations because of its tremendous number of field personnel stationed in areas likely to contain wetlands. Nonetheless, the Corps has identified "surveillance" as an appropriate method using Corps employees, members of the public, and representatives of state, local, and other federal agencies,[246] and "inspections" of permitted activities by Corps personnel, members of the public, and interested state, local, and other federal agency representatives "encouraging" them to report suspected violations.[247]

---

[242] Enforcement MOA, ¶III.D.2-4.

[243] Enforcement MOA, ¶III.D.4.

[244] 33 U.S.C. §§1319(a)(5) and 1344(s); 33 C.F.R. §326.3(d).

[245] Enforcement MOA, ¶II.A.

[246] 33 C.F.R. §326.3(a).

[247] 33 C.F.R. §326.4(a).

CIVIL ENFORCEMENT

The Enforcement MOA requires the Corps and the Environmental Protection Agency to follow five predetermined procedural steps once an unpermitted violation is discovered.[248] First, in the initial investigatory stage, the Corps's field investigation report is prepared after it has checked with the Environmental Protection Agency to make sure that it has not already begun an investigation.[249] Once a violation is found, the field investigation report shall include at least a detailed description of the illegal activity, the existing environmental setting, an initial description of potential impacts, and a recommendation of the need for corrective measures.[250] Second, after preparation of the report, the investigating agency must notify the violator to inform them to cease their illegal activity pending further federal action.[251] The input from other agencies may be considered at this early stage if time permits.[252] In addition, the investigating agency shall notify the other agency of its violation letters and request the other

---

[248] Enforcement MOA, ¶III.A. Attached to the Enforcement MOA is a flowchart of procedures which, the text states, may be "combined in an effort to expedite the enforcement process". The only exception to the procedure is when the unpermitted activity occurs in a specially-defined geographic area over which the Environmental Protection Agency has already asserted exclusive jurisdiction under the *Memorandum of Agreement Between the Department of the Army and the Environmental Protection Agency Concerning the Determination of the Geographic Jurisdiction of the Section 404 Program and the Application of the Exemption Under Section 404(f) of the Clean Water Act* (January 19, 1989), ¶V.A.

[249] 33 C.F.R. §326.3(g).

[250] Enforcement MOA, ¶III.B. 33 C.F.R. §326.3(b) also requires the Corps to "confirm whether a violation exists, and if so, . . . identify the extent of the violation and the parties responsible".

[251] Enforcement MOA, ¶III.C. The Corps can issue a cease and desist order at this stage for uncompleted projects. 33 C.F.R. §326.3(c)(1). In other appropriate cases, the Corps may "allow the work to continue, subject to appropriate limitations and conditions". *Id.*

[252] *Id.*; Further, the Corps and the Environmental Protection Agency are "encouraged to enter into interagency agreements with other federal, state, tribal and local agencies which will provide assistance to the Corps and EPA in pursuit of Section 404 enforcement activities". Enforcement MOA, ¶IV.A.

agency's views and recommendations on the case.[253]

The third step, selection of the lead enforcement agency, has already been discussed above. Briefly repeated, the Environmental Protection Agency will take the unpermitted activity cases involving repeat violators, flagrant violations, request by the Environmental Protection Agency, or referral from the Corps. The Corps will take the remaining unpermitted activity cases as well as the permit condition violation cases.[254]

After selecting the lead enforcement agency, it shall determine the appropriate enforcement response which may include an administrative order, administrative penalty complaint, a civil or criminal referral to the Department of Justice, or any other appropriate formal enforcement response.[255] Having made up its mind on the appropriate enforcement response, the lead enforcement agency shall arrange for monitoring if it required corrective measures or removal, make its final determination that the violation is resolved, and so notify the other agency unless the decision has been made to refer the violation to the Department of Justice.[256] If the case will involve further administrative enforcement actions or further remedial measures the failure to comply with which will later result in legal action, the Corps's regulations require that it keep its case open.[257]

Referrals to the Department of Justice are made when "appropriate" which the Corps's regulations define as violations which are "willful, repeated, flagrant, or of substantial impact".[258] If the Department of Justice declines to take the case, the local

---

[253] *Id.*

[254] Enforcement MOA, ¶III.D.

[255] Enforcement MOA, ¶III.E; In addition, the Corps is specifically prohibited from accepting application for "after-the-fact" permits until the lead enforcement agency has "resolved" the violation. Enforcement MOA, ¶III.G and 33 C.F.R. §326.3(e).

[256] Enforcement MOA, ¶III.F.

[257] 33 C.F.R. §326.5(a).

[258] 33 C.F.R. §326.5(a). There is no requirement that the Corps or Environmental Protection Agency follow either the Administrative Penalty process (Chapter 7, above) or proceed directly to

district engineer may either close the enforcement case or, if the case warrants special attention, then the district engineer is "encouraged" to forward a litigation report to the Office, Chief of Engineers.[259]

If the Department of Justice does decide to take the case, it may seek a number of different remedies in the federal district court in which the defendant resides, is located, or does business, including injunctive relief commanding the alleged violator to cease his or her violation or to restore the wetland to its pre-violation condition.[260] In addition, courts are permitted to assess civil penalties of their own.[261]

There is no specific statute of limitations under the Clean Water Act but the

---

judicial enforcement. *United States v. Earth Sciences, Inc.*, 599 F.2d 368 (10th Cir. Colo. 1979).

[259] 33 C.F.R. §326.5(e).

[260] See e.g., *United States v. Bayshore Associates, Inc.*, 934 F.2d 1391 (6th Cir. Mich. 1991); *United States v. Rivera Torres*, 656 F.Supp. 251 (D.P.R. 1986), *aff'd*, 826 F.2d 151 (1st Cir. P.R. 1987); *United States v. Tilton*, 705 F.2d 429 (11th Cir. Fla. 1983); *United States v. Leuzen*, 816 F.Supp. 1171 (S.D.Tex. 1993); *United States v. Malibu Beach, Inc.*, 711 F.Supp. 1301 (D.N.J. 1989); *United States v. Larkins*, 657 F.Supp. 76 (W.D.Ky. 1987), *aff'd.*, 852 F.2d 189 (6th Cir. Ky. 1988), *cert. denied*, 489 U.S. 1016, 101 L.Ed.2d 193, 109 S.Ct. 1131 (1989); *United States v. Lambert*, 589 F.Supp. 366 (M.D.Fla. 1984); *United States v. Robinson*, 570 F.Supp. 1157 (M.D.Fla. 1983); *United States v. Bradshaw*, 541 F.Supp. 884 (D.Md. 1982); *United States v. Weisman*, 489 F.Supp. 1331 (M.D.Fla. 1980); *United States v. D'Annolfo*, 474 F.Supp. 220 (D.Mass. 1979). But see *United States v. Huebner*, 752 F.2d 1235 (7th Cir.), *cert. denied*, 474 U.S. 817, 88 L.Ed.2d 50, 106 S.Ct. 62 (1985); *United States v. Sexton Cove Estates, Inc.*, 526 F.2d 1293 (5th Cir. 1976).

[261] 33 U.S.C. §1319(d). The court's maximum penalty is $25,000 per day for each violation. Each day a violation is in place has been held to be a separate violation. *United States v. Cumberland Farms of Connecticut, Inc.*, *supra* (civil penalty forgiven if restoration project is completed); *United States v. Tull*, 615 F.Supp. 610 (E.D.Va. 1983), *aff'd*, 769 F.2d 182 (4th Cir. 1985), *rev'd on other grounds sub nom. Tull v. United States*, 481 U.S. 412, 95 L.Ed.2d 365, 107 S.Ct. 1831 (1987) (in *Tull*, the defendant admitted that he had placed fill in four locations but denied that the properties were wetlands; the government sought the maximum penalty of $22,890,000; the trial court found that the properties were wetlands, ordered Mr. Tull to restore those properties which he had not yet sold, awarded the government $75,000 in outright civil penalties, and ordered a suspended additional civil penalty of $250,000 on the condition that one of the properties be restored to its former navigable condition, which Mr.Tull discovered would require him to purchase additional property which cost $700,000); *United States v. Ciampitti*, 669 F.Supp. 684 (D.N.J. 1987), *aff'd*, 772 F.2d 893 (3d Cir. N.J. 1985), *cert. denied sub nom. Ciampitti v. United States*, 475 U.S. 1014, 89 L.Ed.2d 307, 106 S.Ct. 1192 (1986).

courts apply the five-year limitations period for civil penalty actions.[262] Defendants have a right to a jury trial on the issue of liability, although the court will decide the amount of civil penalty and the terms of an injunction.[263]

CRIMINAL ENFORCEMENT

In addition to civil penalties, under §309©[264] of the Clean Water Act, the Environmental Protection Agency has pursued criminal sanctions against violators in cases involving extreme conduct, such as refusing to obey cease and desist orders, or drastic harm to wetlands. Some cases have involved a combination of civil penalties and criminal sanctions. The criminal penalty for negligent violations is a fine of not less than $2,500 nor more than $25,000 per day of violation, or by imprisonment for not more than one year, or both.[265] Knowing violations are punishable by a fine of not less than $5,000 nor more than $50,000 per day of violation, or by imprisonment for not more than three years, or both.[266] False statements on permit applications and tampering with monitoring devices may draw a fine of not more than $10,000, or imprisonment

---

[262] 28 U.S.C. §2462. *Sasser v. EPA*, 990 F.2d 127 (4th Cir. 1993); *United States v. Windward Properties, Inc.*, 821 F.Supp. 690 N.D.Ga.1993); *United States v. Hobbs*, 736 F.Supp. 1406 (E.D.Va. 1990); *Public Interest Research Group of New Jersey v. Powell Duffryn Terminals, Inc.*, 913 F.2d 64 (3d Cir. N.J. 1990), *cert. denied*, 498 U.S. 1109, 112 L.Ed.2d 1100, 111 S.Ct. 1018 (1991); *Atlantic States Legal Foundation, Inc. v. Al Tech Specialty Steel Corp.*, 635 F.Supp. 284 (N.D.N.Y. 1986).

[263] *United States v. M.C.C. of Florida, Inc.* 848 F.2d 1133 (11th Cir. 1988), *reh'g granted*, 863 F.2d 802 (11th Cir. Fla. 1989), *appeal after remand*, 967 F.2d 1559 (11 Cir. Fla. 1992); *United States v. Key West Towers, Inc.*, 720 F.Supp. 963 (S.D.Fla. 1989).

[264] 33 U.S.C. §1319(c).

[265] 33 U.S.C. §1319(c)(1). If the defendant has one or more Clean Water Act convictions on his or her record already, the maximum amount of the fine and the jail term are both doubled.

[266] 33 U.S.C. §1319(c)(2). For persons with one or more previous convictions, the fine may not exceed $100,000 per day of violation, and the jail term is not more than six years, or both.

for not more than two years, or both.[267]

The courts have ordered some fairly severe fines and sentences. For example, in *United States v. Pozgai*,[268] despite many warnings and entry of a temporary restraining order of which he had already been held in contempt, Mr. Pozgai was finally sentenced to three years in prison. In *United States v. Ellen*[269], the project manager was sentenced to six months in jail. Violators and potential violators should be advised that criminal sanctions are a real possibility and have been applied with increasing frequency in recent years.

CITIZEN SUITS

Although private citizens cannot sue for damages under either the Rivers and Harbors Act of 1899 or the Clean Water Act because there is no general private right of action,[270] they can sue the United States, the Environmental Protection Agency, and/or the Corps for an unpermitted discharge of fill material in a wetland, a wrongful permit issuance, and erroneous determinations of wetlands jurisdiction,[271] and can seek equitable relief in the form of an injunction directly against violators. Jurisdiction in

---

[267]   33 U.S.C. §1319(c)(4). Multiple prior convictions double the fine and jail term.

[268]   *United States v. Pozgai*, № 88-00450 (E.D.Pa. December 30, 1988), *aff'd*, 897 F.2d 524 (3d Cir.), *cert. denied*, 498 U.S. 812, 112 L.Ed.2d 24, 111 S.Ct. 48 (1990).

[269]   *United States v. Ellen*, 961 F.2d 462 (4th Cir. Md. 1992), *cert. denied*, 121 L.Ed.2d 155 (1992).

[270]   *Middlesex County Sewerage Authority v. National Sea Clammers Association*, 453 U.S. 1 (1981) (no private right of action under the Clean Water Act); *California v. Sierra Club*, 451 U.S. 287 (1981) (no private right of action under the Rivers and Harbors Act of 1899).

[271]   33 U.S.C. §§1365(a)(1) and 1365(f); *Vieux Carre Property Owners, Residents & Assocs. v. Brown*, 875 F.2d 453 (5th Cir. La. 1989), *cert. denied*, 493 U.S. 1020, 107 L.Ed.2d 739, 110 S.Ct. 720 (1990); *Orleans Audubon Society v. Lee*, 742 F.2d 901 (5th Cir.), *reh'g denied*, 750 F.2d 69 (5th Cir. La. 1984); *Hough v. Marsh*, 557 F.Supp. 74 (D.Mass. 1982). See also 68 ALR Fed. 701, §5.

the federal courts is authorized by the general federal question statute[272] and, under the Clean Water Act only, a special citizens' suit provision.[273] Venue is proper only in the district in which the "source is located", i.e., usually but not necessarily where the wetland is located.[274] If the citizen suit seeks monetary penalties, the statute of limitations is five years from the date on which knowledge of the violation was first obtained, rather than the date of the violation itself.[275] If, however, the suit seeks equitable relief, there is no statute of limitations although there is some authority that the citizen suit cannot be maintained for "wholly-past" violations.[276] Of course, the citizen suit must be an actual case or controversy under Article III of the U.S. Constitution meaning that plaintiff must have standing to bring the action by showing individualized harm.[277]

Prior to actually filing a citizen suit, plaintiff is required to give a notice of intent to sue to the violator, the Administrator of the Environmental Protection Agency (and, although not specifically mentioned, to the Secretary of the Army as well), and to the state in which the wetland is located.[278] This notice is mandatory and, therefore, jurisdictional.[279] The purpose of the notice is to provide the government an opportunity

---

[272]   28 U.S.C. §1331.

[273]   33 U.S.C. §1365.

[274]   33 U.S.C. §1365(c).

[275]   28 U.S.C. §2462; *United States v. Hobbs*, 736 F.Supp. 1406 (E.D.Va. 1990).

[276]   *Gwaltney of Smithfield v. Chesapeake Bay Foundation*, 484 U.S. 49 (1987). In wetland cases, a continuing violation can be found from the continued existence of the fill in the wetland, as opposed to some historic single-event discharge of a pollutant.

[277]   *Cane Creek Conservation Authority v. Orange Water Authority*, 590 F.Supp. 1123 (M.D.N.C. 1984).

[278]   33 U.S.C. §1365(b).

[279]   See 40 C.F.R. §§135.1, 135.2, and 135.3 for the service and content requirements of the notice. See also *National Environmental Foundation v. ABC Rail Corporation*, 926 F.2d 1096 (11th Cir. Ala. 1991); *Canada Community Improvement Society, Inc. v. Michigan City*, 742 F.Supp. 1025

to bring its own enforcement action[280] as citizen suits were never intended to take the place of government enforcement actions,[281] but only as an aid in the protection of the environment.[282] If, however, the government declines to take action within the sixty-day notice period, then the citizen must also serve a copy of his or her complaint on the government to allow it to monitor the citizen suit for potential abuse.[283] Another limitation on the availability of citizen suits is that they cannot be used to force the government to take enforcement action, which has been held repeatedly to be a "discretionary", as opposed to a "mandatory", duty of the government.[284]

A final problem in maintaining a citizen suit is what to do with the monetary penalties once the suit has been successful. Obviously it would do little to advance the cause of protecting the environment if private citizens could keep the penalty award. Generally, the funds should be used for environmental improvement projects, either directly or indirectly related to the violation.[285]

(N.D.Ind. 1990).

[280] 33 U.S.C. §1365(b)(1)(B) (which prohibits the maintenance of a citizen suit if the federal or state government "has commenced and is diligently prosecuting a civil or criminal action".
Citizens still maintain a right to intervene in the government action. For discussion of the meaning of "diligently prosecuting", see *Atlantic States Legal Foundation v. Universal Tool & Stamping Company* 735 F.Supp. 1404 (N.D.Ind. 1990); *New York Public Interest Research Group v. Limco Manufacturing Corporation*, 697 F.Supp. 608 (E.D.N.Y. 1987); *Connecticut Fund for the Environment v. Job Plating Company*, 623 F.Supp. 207 (D.Conn. 1985).

[281] *Save Our Sound Fisheries Association v. Callaway*, 429 F.Supp. 1136 (D.R.I. 1977).

[282] *Pennsylvania Environmental Defense Foundation v. Bellefonte Borough*, 718 F.Supp. 431 (M.D.Pa. 1989).

[283] 40 C.F.R. §135.4.

[284] *Harmon Cove Condominium Association, Inc. v, Marsh*, 815 F.2d 949 (3d Cir. N.J. 1987); *Sierra Club v. Train*, 557 F.2d 485 (5th Cir. Ala. 1977); *National Wildlife Federation v. Laubscher*, 662 F.Supp. 548 (S.D.Tex. 1987). See also the Federal Administrative Procedure Act, 5 U.S.C. §500 *et seq.* for distinction between maintenance of suits by private individuals to compel the government's performance of mandatory, as opposed to discretionary, duties. See also 57 ALR Fed. 851, §§2 and 7.

[285] *Sierra Club v. Electronic Controls Design, Inc.*, 703 F.Supp. 875 (D.Or. 1989), *rev'd. on other grounds and remanded*, 909 F.2d 1350 (9th Cir. Ore. 1990).

CHAPTER NINE
LITIGATION AND DEFENSES

Litigation under the Clean Water Act will arise in one of three ways: (1) the Corps or Environmental Protection Agency may refer their enforcement case to the Department of Justice; or (2) a private citizen (which may be an individual person, a corporation, or an environmental group) may bring an enforcement action against either the Corps or the Environmental Protection Agency, or both, and the alleged violator; or (3) a permit applicant may be somehow unhappy with the outcome of the permit application, alleging either that its denial was unlawful or the conditions imposed upon its grant work too great a hardship. Section 505 of the Clean Water Act allows private citizen suits against the Environmental Protection Agency for failure to perform "non-discretionary acts".[286] The Corps may be joined as a party defendant under a number of theories despite the fact that suits against it are not specifically authorized by §505.[287]

Although there is generally no judicial review of a governmental agency's refusal to pursue enforcement measures,[288] one recent case permitted a private suit for monetary damages under the Federal Tort Claims Act.[289] In *Hurst* the plaintiff became aware of permit violations in a project upstream from his property. He notified the Corps which investigated and conceded that violations were occurring. Nonetheless the

---

[286] 33 U.S.C. §1365.

[287] See *National Wildlife Federation v. Hanson*, 859 F.2d 313 (4th Cir. N.C. 1988) (Corps may be joined when it fails to make a reasonable wetlands determination); *Golden Gate Audubon Society, Inc. v. U.S. Army Corps of Engineers*, 18 Envtl.L.Rep. 21401 (N.D.Cal. 1988) (Corps may be sued under the Administrative Procedure Act, 5 U.S.C. §500 *et seq.*).

[288] See Chapter 8, above.

[289] *Hurst v. United States*, 882 F.2d 306 (8th Cir. S.D. 1989).

Corps took no enforcement action and, as a consequence of the violations, plaintiff's property was flooded. In that case the court was persuaded that once the Corps becomes aware of a permit violation, enforcement is no longer considered "discretionary" at least as far as after the fact damage caused by the violation.

In a private citizen suit for enforcement there are two additional factual thresholds for plaintiff to cross: (1) it must have standing to sue, i.e., be an "aggrieved person"; and, (2) the violation must be ongoing in the present. "Standing" is a concept which basically requires that the proper person bring the lawsuit. In the context of Clean Water Act litigation, "standing" requires that only those persons who actually use the affected area, will be significantly affected, or will suffer a particular individualized harm from the government action may sue.[290] The limitation in which citizen suits cannot be heard for wholly-past violations is weak and easily overcome.[291]

PROCEDURAL ISSUES

Ripeness

Since private persons have no right of direct administrative appeal of the Corps's permit decisions,[292] they may "appeal" by filing a new lawsuit in federal court.

---

[290] *Cane Creek Conservation Authority v. Orange Water Authority*, 590 F.Supp. 1123 (M.D.N.C. 1984).

[291] See Chapter 8, above.

[292] Pre-enforcement review is barred thus a property owners who is not happy with a permit decision is forced to violate the permit, draw and enforcement proceeding against him or her, and only then seek judicial review of the underlying enforcement decision. *Southern Pines Associates v. United States*, 912 F.2d 713 (4th Cir. Va. 1990); *Hoffman Group Inc. v. U.S. Environmental Protection Agency*, 902 F.2d 567 (7th Cir. 1990); *Hampton Venture No. One v. United States*, 768 F.Supp. 174 (E.D.Va. 1991); *Route 26 Land Development Association v. United States*, 753 F.Supp. 532 (D.Del. 1990), *aff'd.* 961 F.2d 1568 (3d Cir. Del. 1992); *Fercom Aquaculture Corp. v. United States*, 740

(continued...)

Jurisdiction is proper in federal court because a claim under the Clean Water Act presents a federal question.[293] However, the case must be "ripe" prior to filing such a suit.

"Ripeness" is a doctrine applied by the courts to prevent premature lawsuits. In other words, the controversy must have reached a certain stage of disagreement such that there is something for the court to adjudicate, i.e., a so-called justiciable actual controversy under Article III of the U.S. Constitution. Before that stage is reached, courts say that a case is not "ripe", and that the court therefore lacks jurisdiction to decide it.

The issue of ripeness arises frequently in cases involving judicial review of administrative decisions. In Clean Water Act litigation, the doctrine of ripeness requires first of all that the regulation is question must actually be applied against the landowner rather than merely enacted as a potential regulation in a hypothetical set of circumstances. The Corps must have actually determined that the property is a wetland or taken some action toward the landowner based upon that determination: usually either a permit denial or an enforcement action, or the reverse in a citizen suit. The landowner would then seek either a declaratory judgment that the wetlands determination is improper or incorrect, or an injunction to prohibit an enforcement action, or the private citizen would allege that the wetlands determination was erroneous and, consequently, a permit should have been denied or conditioned. In considering whether a case is "ripe" or not, these administrative determinations must be complete and final. If they are not, the case is not ripe. Particularly in cases in which the private landowner complains that his land has been "taken" by the government by virtue of a denial of a permit, the landowner must first show that he properly applied

---

[292](...continued)
F.Supp. 736 (E.D.Mo. 1990); *USI Properties Corp. v. U.S. Environmental Protection Agency*, 517 F.Supp. 1235 (D.P.R. 1981).

[293]   28 U.S.C. §1331.

for the permit and that it was in fact denied.[294] The court is then relieved of the potential responsibility of making a wetland determination itself and can concentrate instead on the legal propriety of the permit grant or denial or enforcement action. As the Supreme Court stated in *Riverside Bayview Homes*, the ". . . requirement that a person obtain a permit before engaging in a certain use of his or her property does not itself 'take' the property in any sense: after all, the very existence of the permit system implies that permission may be granted, leaving the landowner free to use the property as desired. Moreover, even if the permit is denied, there may be other viable uses available to the owner".[295]

Judicial Review of Administrative Decisions

Another threshold procedural issue, sometimes stated separately but in reality a corollary of the concept of ripeness, is the general prohibition against judicial review of administrative decisions until the administrative decision is complete and final, including the requirement that the person complaining about the administrative decision must have availed himself of every avenue of remedy within the administrative agency before coming to court (called "exhaustion of administrative remedies"). Even then, that the judicial review must be limited to the record generated

---

[294] *United States v. Riverside Bayview Homes*, 474 U.S. 121, 88 L.Ed.2d 419, 106 S.Ct. 455 (1985); *Williamson County Regional Planning Commission v. Hamilton Bank*, 473 U.S. 172, 87 L.Ed.2d 126, 105 S.Ct. 3108 (1985); *Hodel v. Virginia Surface Mining Reclamation Ass'n.*, 452 U.S. 264, 69 L.Ed.2d 1, 101 S.Ct. 2352 (1981). As the Supreme Court stated in *Williamson*, ". . . a claim that the application of government regulations effects a taking of a property interest is not ripe until the government entity charged with implementing the regulations has reached a final decision regarding application of the regulations to the property at issue". *Hamilton*, 473 U.S. at 186.

[295] *U.S. v. Riverside Bayview Homes, supra.* See also *Danforth v. United States*, 308 U.S. 271, 84 L.Ed.2d 240, 60 S.Ct. 231 (1939), in which the mere enactment of a flood control statute was not a taking because "such legislation may be repealed or modified, or appropriations may fail", and *Willink v. United States*, 240 U.S. 572, 60 L.Ed. 808, 36 S.Ct. 422 (1916).

in the administrative proceeding.[296] An administrative agency such as the Corps possesses specialized knowledge and is considered to be in the best position to make an accurate administrative decision based upon the facts before it. More so, at least, than the reviewing court. The court's role is supposed to be limited to reviewing the administrative record to determine whether the administrative agency's determination or enforcement action was "arbitrary and capricious".[297]

This concept of exhaustion of administrative remedies coupled with the limitation of review to the administrative record may be more honored in the breach since it embraces two components, both of which *should* be satisfied prior to judicial review: completeness and finality. Whether the administrative decision was based upon a complete record can be difficult to determine. At this stage in the development of the case law it is difficult to derive a hard and fast rule with respect to the Clean Water Act because litigation concerning it frequently involves the application of other, additional statutes which skew the judicial results.

If one starts with the basic rule that the court is limited in its review to the administrative record before it,[298] in cases involving wetlands determinations under the Clean Water Act an immediate problem arises: the "record" may be virtually non-existent because the wetland determination and consequent assertion of jurisdiction may have been based only upon an informal site visit in which very little documentation was produced. In litigation concerning an improper grant of a permit, in addition to application of the Clean Water Act, the National Environmental Policy Act may apply which under certain circumstances requires the production of an environmental assessment or an environmental impact statement which may itself be inadequate or nonexistent.

---

[296] *Avoyelles Sportmen's League, Inc. v. Marsh*, 715 F.2d 897 (5th Cir. La. 1983).

[297] 5 U.S.C. §706(2)(a).

[298] *Avoyelles Sportmen's League, Inc. v. Marsh, supra.; Bailey v. United States*, 647 F.Supp. 44 (D.Idaho (1986); *Shoreline Associates v. Marsh*, 555 F.Supp. 169 (D.Md. 1983), *aff'd*, 725 F.2d 677 (4th Cir. Md. 1984).

In this situation the courts have two options: they may either remand the case back to the Corps with instructions to generate an adequate record for the court to review; or, they may proceed to review that case anyway under the National Environmental Policy Act to determine the adequacy of the environmental assessment or environmental impact statement if one was required to be prepared. Which option the court will select has, at least historically, been dependent upon whether the underlying dispute involves merely a wetlands determination or a final grant or denial of a permit.

If the case involves merely a wetlands determination, in the majority of cases so far, the courts limit their consideration to the administrative record.[299] If the record is inadequate, the courts remand the case back to the Corps to generate a better record.[300] Nonetheless, one lower court has received new evidence beyond the scope of the administrative record in a wetlands determination case.[301]

If the case involves the grant of a permit, the majority of courts still limit their review to the administrative record. In this situation there is more likely to be an adequate administrative record generated by the procedures outlined above. However, if the case *also* involves an allegation that an environmental assessment or environmental impact statement should have been prepared under the National Environmental Policy Act, or that the environmental assessment or environmental impact statement that was prepared is somehow inadequate, then the courts *may* allow additional evidence though even this additional evidence is limited to the scope of the administrative record.[302]

---

[299]   *Avoyelles Sportmen's League v. Marsh, supra.*

[300]   *National Wildlife Federation v. Hanson, supra.*

[301]   *Leslie Salt Co. v. U.S.*, 700 F.Supp. 476 (N.D.Cal. 1988), *reversed on other grounds.*, 20 Envtl.L.Rep. 20477 (9th Cir. 1990).

[302]   *Louisiana Wildlife Federation v. York*, 603 F.Supp. 518 (W.D.La. 1984), *aff'd in part and vacated in part*, 761 F.2d 1044 (5th Cir. La. 1985).

If the case involves the denial of a permit and the private landowner alleges that the effect of a permit denial is a taking of his property such that the Fifth Amendment of the U.S. Constitution requires that he or she be paid just compensation,[303] these procedural thresholds take on additional significance. Exhaustion of administrative remedies becomes more important because in order to show a taking, the landowner must show not only that his or her first plan drew a permit denial, but that all plans he or she might submit would also draw a permit denial thus there is no economically viable use left in the property[304] and that all administrative procedures to obtain compensation have been exhausted.[305] Whether the landowner has exhausted his or her administrative remedies and whether the Corps's decision is complete and final can be a difficult threshold to cross. For example, how many plans must the developer submit? Has he or she submitted every conceivable development plan such that denial of all of them deprives the landowner of all economically viable use? Certainly this procedural threshold would require the submission of at least two plans: the first which was denied, and a second attempt.[306] The reason for this "final and authoritative" determination requirement is that the court cannot figure out if a regulation goes "too far" without knowing to what extent the regulation will be applied. To make that determination, the court has to know with some specificity the nature of the activity

---

[303]   See "The Fifth Amendment Taking Defense", below.

[304]   *MacDonald, Sommer & Frates v. Yolo County*, 477 U.S. 340, 91 L.Ed.2d 285, 106 S.Ct. 2561 (1986), *reh'g. denied*, 478 U.S. 1035, 92 L.Ed.2d 773, 107 S.Ct. 22 (1986); *Williamson County Regional Planning Commission v. Hamilton Bank*, 473 U.S. 172, 87 L.Ed.2d 126, 105 S.Ct. 3108 (1985); *Ruckelshaus v. Monsanto*, 467 U.S. 986, 81 L.Ed.2d 815, 104 S.Ct. 2862 (1984); *Hodel v. Virginia Surface Mining & Reclamation Association*, 452 U.S. 264, 69 L.Ed.2d 1, 101 S.Ct. 2352 (1981); *Agins v. City of Tiburon*, 447 U.S. 255, 65 L.Ed.2d 106, 100 S.Ct. 2138 (1980); *Penn Central Transportation Co. v. New York City*, 438 U.S. 104, 57 L.Ed.2d 631, 98 S.Ct. 2646 (1978), *reh'g. denied*, 439 U.S. 883, 58 L.Ed.2d 198, 99 S.Ct. 226 (1978).

[305]   *Williamson County Regional Planning Commission v. Hamilton Bank, supra.*

[306]   *MacDonald, Sommer & Frates v. Yolo County, supra*; *Williamson County Regional Planning Commission v. Hamilton Bank, supra.*; *Agins v. City of Tiburon, supra*; *Penn Central Transportation Co. v. New York City, supra.*

being limited or prohibited by the permit denial. In addition, the potential plaintiff must have applied for every other permit which might conceivably be applicable so that the court can determine which permit denial was the culprit causing the taking if one occurred.[307] There is also an issue of how long the potential plaintiff should spend submitting these additional development plans. Temporary takings are recognized[308] during the period of time the administrative process was ongoing, but the courts have been fairly generous in allowing time for the permit application process.[309]

Statute Of Limitations

The courts have applied the general six-year statute of limitations[310] to suits against the Corps and the Environmental Protection Agency arising out of their permit decisions. This limitation period should be distinguished from the five-year limitations period for civil enforcement suits brought by the Corps or Environmental Protection Agency against permit violators or for unpermitted discharges.

---

[307] There is a futility exception espoused by a few lower courts in which, under certain facts, the requirement of submitting a second plan or applying for other required permits may be waived if, under an extreme set of facts, it would be futile to do so.

[308] *First English Evangelical Lutheran Church of Glendale v. County of Los Angeles*, 493 U.S. 1056, 107 L.Ed.2d 950, 110 S.Ct. 866 (1990), in which an ordinance barred reconstruction in a flood zone. The Supreme Court held that assuming that the ordinance worked a taking, compensation should be paid during the time the ordinance was in effect.

[309] In one case the plaintiffs wished to develop a 112-acre parcel but it took the Corps 16 months to decide which 70 acres of the parcel was the wetland. *Dufau v. United States*, 22 Cl.Ct. 156 (1990). While the plaintiffs were waiting for their wetland determination and permit, the bottom fell out of the real estate market to the extent that when they finally did get their permit, there was no one to buy the lots. They claimed a temporary taking during the permit application process. The court rejected their claim. Perhaps compelling to the court was a finding that some of the delay had been caused by the plaintiffs themselves. *Dufau* teaches that not only must the potential plaintiff submit additional proposals, he or she must be diligent and timely about these additional efforts as well. See also *1902 Atlantic, Ltd.* v. Hudson, 574 F.Supp. 1381 (E.D.Va. 1983).

[310] 28 U.S.C. §2401(a).

LIABILITY

In enforcement actions brought by the government, §404 of the Clean Water Act and §10 of the Rivers and Harbors Act of 1899 provide for strict liability even to the extent of piercing the corporate veil and holding officers liable if they participated in the violation.[311] In addition to enforcement actions against the property owner, other persons who assisted in the violation may also be held liable.[312]

ATTORNEYS FEES

Attorneys fees and expert witness fees are allowed for any prevailing or substantially prevailing party under §505(d) of the Clean Water Act.[313]

THE FIFTH AMENDMENT TAKING DEFENSE

The Fifth Amendment taking defense has only very recently emerged in wetlands cases with varying success. It is not precisely a defense since its successful outcome against the government does not alter the Corps's wetland determination or permit denial or conditioning. Instead, the plaintiff will receive money but lose his or her property. Of the remaining defenses asserted, so few have been successful, and

---

[311]   *United States v. Pollution Abatement Services of Oswego*, 763 F. 2d 133 (2d Cir. N.Y. 1985), *cert. denied sub nom. Miller v. U.S.*, 474 U.S. 1037, 88 L.Ed.2d 583, 106 S.Ct. 605 (1985).

[312]   *United States v. Pollution Abatement Services of Oswego, Inc., supra.*; *United States v. Board of Trustees of Florida Keys Community College*, 531 F.Supp. 267 (S.D.Fla. 1981). But see *United States v. Sexton Cove Estates, Inc.*, 526 F.2d 1293 (5th Cir. Fla. 1976); *United States v. Joseph G. Moretti, Inc.*, 526 F.2d 1306 (5th Cir. Fla. 1976).

[313]   33 U.S.C. §1365(d).

among the successful ones, their application is so limited to the special facts of each individual case that it may be fairly said that liability under the Clean Water Act is truly strict liability, with only a Fifth Amendment claim available to ameliorate the effects of what the Corps intended to do in the first place—make a wetlands determination and/or deny a permit.

The United States Court of Claims held in two cases that a Clean Water Act permit denial for wetlands development was a governmental taking of property for which just compensation must be paid[314] to the property-owning permit applicant.[315] These two cases sent a shiver down the spine of environmentalists because they appeared to expand the criteria for finding a taking far beyond the modern criteria for analyzing taking cases developed over the past seventy years. The sense of the environmentalist community was that these cases would have a chilling effect on the Corps's otherwise orthodox enforcement of the Clean Water Act because the Corps would have to demur from enforcing the Clean Water Act to avoid the risk of paying considerable sums of money damages for denying a permit to develop land.[316] In Congress *Florida Rock Industries* and *Loveladies Harbor* spawned a flurry of bills[317]

---

[314] The Fifth Amendment to the United States Constitution provides in relevant part ". . . nor shall private property be taken for public use, without just compensation.".

[315] *Loveladies Harbor, Inc. v. United States*, 28 F.3d 1171 (Fed. Cir. 1994), *reh'g. denied en banc*, 1994 U.S. App. LEXIS 28462 (Fed. Cir. September 29, 1994); *Florida Rock Industries, Inc. v. United States*, 21 Cl.Ct. 161 (1990), *cert. denied*, 130 L.Ed.2d 783, 115 S.Ct. 898 (1995).

[316] These fears were not unjustified. See *Lucas v. South Carolina Coastal Council*, 120 L.Ed.2d 798, 112 S.Ct. 2886 (1992); *Formanek v. United States*, 26 Cl.Ct. 332 (1992).

[317] See e.g., Senate Bill 50, the "Private Property Rights Act of 1990", which states in relevant part the "(n)o regulation promulgated after the date of enactment of this Act by any agency shall become effective until the issuing agency is certified by the Attorney General to be in compliance with Executive Order 12630 or similar procedures to assess the potential for the taking of private property in the course of Federal regulatory activity, with the goal of minimizing such where possible.". Other "anti-taking" bills included, in 1991, H.R. 1572, the "Private Property Rights Act of 1991", H.R. 1650, H.R. 3092, and H.R. 905; in 1992, H.R. Res. 404, H.R.Res. 1330, S.B. 1463, and H.R. 1330; and, in 1995, H.R. 961, which passed the House by a 2-to-1 vote.

perhaps as much as to bolster an existing Executive Order[318] as to respond to these cases and an earlier, non-wetland taking case.[319]

---

[318] President Reagan's Executive Order 12630, "Governmental Actions and Interference with Constitutionally Protected Property Rights", March 15, 1988, which states in relevant part . . . Executive departments and agencies shall adhere, to the extent permitted by law, to the following criteria when implementing policies that have takings implications:

(a) When an Executive department or agency requires a private party to obtain a permit in order to undertake a specific use of, or action with respect to, private property, any conditions imposed on the granting of the permit shall:

(1) Serve the same purpose that would have been served by a prohibition of the use or action; and

(2) Substantially advance that purpose.

(b) When a proposed action would place a restriction on a use of private property, the restriction imposed on the use shall not be disproportionate to the extent to which the use contributes to the overall problem that the restriction is imposed to redress.

© When a proposed action involves a permitting process or any other decision making process that will interfere with, or otherwise prohibit, the use of private property pending completion of the process, the duration of the process shall be kept to the minimum necessary.

(d) Before undertaking any proposed action regulating private property use for the protection of public health or safety, the Executive department or agency involved shall, in internal deliberative documents and any submissions to the Director of the Office of Management and Budget that are required:

(1) Identify clearly, with as much specificity as possible, the public health or safety risk created by the private property use that is the subject of the proposed action;

(2) Establish that such proposed action substantially advances the purpose of protecting public health and safety against the specifically identified risk;

(3) Establish to the extent possible that the restrictions imposed on the private property are not disproportionate to the extent to which the use contributes to the overall risk; and

(4) Estimate, to the extent possible, the potential cost to the government in the event that a court later determines that the action constituted a taking.

[319] *Nollan v. California Coastal Commission*, 483 U.S. 825, 97 L.Ed.2d 677, 107 S.Ct. 3141 (1987). In *Nollan* the California Coastal Commission conditioned its grant of a construction permit upon the Nollans granting an easement for public passage which ran parallel to but was above the mean high tide line. The CCC's justification for their requirement was that the Nollans construction of their house would block the public's visual access to the beach which necessarily ran perpendicular to the beach. Essentially the Supreme Court found that the requirement of an easement (which it found to be a physical invasion) parallel to the beach to remedy the public's loss of visual access perpendicular to the beach was not reasonably related to the purpose of the statute.

An ancient concept of sovereignty allows a government to limit the uses to which certain land may be put in the public interest by controlling the natural resources found on the land. This concept is now called the public trust doctrine. Under this concept of sovereignty, which may have its roots as far back in time as the first organized society, there is recognized the notion that some natural resources are so important to all of society that no individual private citizen should be able to exclude others from their use. Even though one of the essential elements of private property ownership is the right to exclude others, nonetheless, some "things common to mankind by the law of nature"[320] are so universally important to the survival and prosperity of all that they should remain in common usage and there should be no exclusion of anyone. There is even a modern argument that there is no right of property ownership in the orthodox sense in these natural resources; that they simply cannot be owned by human beings.

Under Roman law these natural resources were held in trust for the public by the sovereign. The English went further saying that the crown actually owned, as opposed to held in trust, tidal navigable waterways.[321] In the United States the doctrine was adopted by the thirteen colonies with each colony holding its individual navigable waterways in trust[322]. With the westward expansion away from the coast line, as the new states were added to the Union, they, too, acquired control over navigable waterways in trust for the public. However, since not all of the navigable waterways in the interior portions of the United States are tidal, the United States included non-

---

[320] This is the Roman law definition, from the Institutes of Justinian, which included air, running water, the sea, and the seashore below high tide line.

[321] Stevens, *The Public Trust: Sovereign's Ancient Prerogative Becomes the People's Environmental Right*, 14 U.C. Davis L.Rev. 195 (1980).

[322] Except for some grants in the Commonwealth of Massachusetts which extend private property ownership down to low tide line instead of high tide line for particular uses.

tidal navigable waterways[323] in its public trust doctrine.[324] In the case of inland, non-tidal navigable waterways, the upper reach of the waterway held in public trust was the ordinary high water line.[325] Recently, some courts have been willing to extend the reach of the lands held in public trust to include the non-navigable tributaries of navigable waterways if the activity in the tributary affects the public trust value in the navigable portion.[326]

Under Roman and English law, the public trust doctrine protected commercial shipping and fishing. In the United States these activities as well as recreational activities, fowling, and drinking and irrigation water needs have been included.[327] As the uses to which water is put have increased, the courts have similarly expanded the interest protected under the public trust doctrine. For example, California now includes lands in their natural state which may serve as ecological study areas, provide food and habitat for birds and marine life, or simply serve to "favorably affect the scenery and climate of the area".[328] Perhaps the most modern expression of the public trust doctrine is that whereas in the past the sovereign held certain lands in trust for certain uses, now there is some discussion that the resources themselves, independent of their human use, may be entitled to protection in their own right.[329]

---

[323] *Martin v. Lessee of Waddell*, 41 U.S. 367, 16 Pet. 367, 10 L.Ed. 997 (1842).

[324] *Pollard v. Hagan*, 44 U.S. 212, 3 How. 212, 11 L.Ed. 565 (1845).

[325] *Barney v. Keokuk*, 94 U.S. 324, 4 Otto 324, 24 L.Ed. 224 (1877).

[326] *National Audubon Society v. Superior Court*, 33 Cal.3d 419, 189 Cal. Rptr. 346, 658 P.2d 709, *cert. denied*, 464 U.S. 977, 78 L.Ed.2d 351, 104 S.Ct. 413 (1983).

[327] *Lamprey v. Metcalf*, 52 Minn. 181, 53 N.W. 1139 (1893).

[328] *Marks v. Whitney*, 6 Cal.3d 251, 98 Cal.Rptr. 790, 491 P.2d 374 (1971).

[329] See Stone, Christopher D., *Should Trees Have Standing? Toward Legal Rights For Natural Objects*, Palo Alto: William Kaufmann, Inc. (1974), p.9. Stone's essay proposes ". . . that we give legal rights to forests, oceans, rivers and other so-called 'natural objects' in the environment—indeed, to the natural environment as a whole." See also Leopold, Aldo, *A Sand County Almanac And Sketches Here and There*, New York: Oxford University Press (American Museum of Natural History Special Members' Edition), 1949 (1968 ed.), pp. 201-226 ("The Land Ethic").

The public trust doctrine would appear to grant authority to the government to take almost any action with respect to private property so long as it could be justified as a measure to protect an essential public resource. Governmental limitations on the use of property under the authority of the Clean Water Act would seem to be a particularly appropriate application of the public trust doctrine in light of the special purpose of the statute, to restore and maintain clean water. Apart from the discussion of whether water itself would have a right to protection, certainly the public's interest in a continued supply of clean water should outweigh an individual's use which fouls it. Indeed some conservationists have taken this middle position, between the water having its own right to protection and the individual's right to do anything he or she chooses with the water present on private property. To some extent the argument was successful until a constitutional principle, the Fifth Amendment Taking Clause, was applied to limit the unfettered application of the public trust doctrine.

As a written legal principle the Taking Clause is nearly 800 years old. Chapter 28 of Magna Carta contains a similar limitation on the unfettered application of sovereignty, perhaps in reaction to King John's abuse of the public trust doctrine to take for himself all the best hunting grounds. Chapter 28 says, directly enough, ". . .(n)o constable or other bailiff of ours shall take anyone's corn or other chattels unless he pays on the spot in cash for them or can delay payment by arrangement with the seller".[330] Two other chapters also require the "agreement" of the property owner before the crown could take property: Chapter 30 promised that ". . .(n)o sheriff, or bailiff of ours, or anyone else shall take the horses or carts of any free man for transport work save with the agreement of that free man.", and Chapter 31 promises ". . .(n)either we nor our bailiffs will take, for castles or other works of ours, timber which is not ours, except with the agreement of him whose timber it is."[331] Obviously the "agreement" contemplated in Chapters 30 and 31 would be forthcoming upon the payment of

---

[330] Encyclopaedia Britannica, 15th ed. 1990, Vol. 7, p. 675.

[331] *Id.*

compensation.

Chapters 28, 30, and 31 did not forbid the crown from ever taking property—the ancient concept of the public trust was preserved—they only require the payment of money or the consent of the owner. Similarly it is important to remember that the Taking Clause does not forbid the government from taking property for public use; it, too, only requires that just compensation be paid.

In order for there to be a "taking" of property by the government[332] triggering the constitutionally-required payment of just compensation, it would seem axiomatic that there must be (a) "property" of some kind, and (b) some form of governmental activity which has the effect of denying property rights. Under the Taking Clause, "property" means more than fee simple ownership of real estate. "Property" as the term is used in Taking Clause cases means "the group of rights inhering in the citizen's relation to the physical thing, as the right to possess, use, and dispose of it".[333] In wetlands cases, the "property" will almost always be an interest in real property, such as fee simple ownership, but it can also include possessory interests such as

---

[332] The Taking Clause applies to the states as well as the federal government by operation of the Due Process Clause in the Fourteenth Amendment. *MacDonald, Sommer & Frates v. County of Yolo, supra,* reaffirming *Chicago, Burlington and Quincy Railroad Co. v. Chicago,* 166 U.S. 226, 41 L.Ed.2d 979, 17 S.Ct. 581 (1897). Further, many state constitutions contain provisions similar to the Taking Clause thus those states' interpretations of their constitutions may also be instructive.

[333] *Ruckleshaus v. Monsanto Co., supra.* In *Ruckelshaus* the property interests alleged to have been taken were trade secrets which the plaintiff was required to disclose to the Environmental Protection Agency in support of an application for a pesticide registration. For a period of time while the application was pending, the Environmental Protection Agency had a duty to keep the information confidential. Instead, it revealed the information. The court found that during the confidentiality-guaranteed period, the government had taken the trade secret.

easements,[334] leaseholds,[335] liens,[336] mineral estates,[337] air space,[338] and water rights.[339] In addition to these traditional ownership or possessory interests in land, it is at least logically possible that some aspects of personal property might be taken in a wetland case, such as the interest of a limited partner in a real estate development partnership that was denied a permit by the Corps.

A "taking" of property will always occur when there is an interference with a

---

[334] *United States v. Welch*, 217 U.S. 333, 54 L.Ed.2d 787 (1910); *United States v. 8.41 Acres of Land*, 680 F.2d 388 (5th Cir. Tex. 1982), *cert. denied*, 479 U.S. 820, 93 L.Ed.2d 38, 107 S.Ct. 85 (1986); *United States v. 2979.72 Acres of Land*, 237 F.2d 165 (4th Cir. Va. 1956); *Redevelopment Agency v. Tobriner*, 153 Cal.App.3d 367, 200 Cal.Rptr. 364, *cert. denied*, 469 U.S. 882, 83 L.Ed.2d 187, 105 S.Ct. 250 (1984).

[335] *Alamo Land & Cattle Co. v. Arizona*, 424 U.S. 295, 47 L.Ed.2d 1, 96 S.Ct. 910 (1976); *Almota Farmers Elevator & Warehouse Co. v. United States*, 409 U.S. 470, 35 L.Ed.2d 1, 93 S.Ct. 791 (1973); *United States v. Pewee Coal Co.*, 341 U.S. 114, 95 L.Ed.2d 809, 71 S.Ct. 670 (1951); *United States v. Westinghouse Electric & Mfg. Co.*, 339 U.S. 261, 94 L.Ed.2d 816, 70 S.Ct. 644 (1950); *United States v. Petty Motor Co.*, 327 U.S. 372, 90 L.Ed.2d 729, 66 S.Ct. 596 (1946), *reh'g. denied*, 327 U.S. 818, 90 L.Ed. 1040, 66 S.Ct. 813 (1946); *United States v. General Motors*, 323 U.S. 373, 89 L.Ed. 311, 65 S.Ct. 357 (1945); *United States v. Right To Use And Occupy 3.38 Acres Of Land*, 484 F.2d 1140 (4th Cir. Va. 1973); *Sun Oil Co. v. United States*, 572 F.2d 786, 215 Cl.Ct. 716 (1978).

[336] *Louisville Joint Stock Land Bank v. Radford*, 295 U.S. 555, 79 L.Ed. 1593, 55 S.Ct. 854 (1935).

[337] *Keystone Bituminous Coal Association v. De Benedictis*, 480 U.S. 470, 94 L.Ed.2d 472, 107 S.Ct. 1232 (1987); *Pennsylvania Coal Co. v. Mahon*, 260 U.S. 393, 67 L.Ed. 322, 43 S.Ct. 158 (1922).

[338] *Griggs v. Allegheny County*, 369 U.S. 84, 7 L.Ed.2d 585, 82 S.Ct. 531, *reh'g. denied*, 369 U.S. 857, 8 L.Ed.2d 16, 82 S.Ct. 931 (1962); *United States v. Causby*, 328 U.S. 256, 90 L.Ed. 1206, 66 S.Ct. 1062 (1946) (which holds that a landowner, in this case a chicken farmer, "owns at least as much of the space above the ground as he can occupy or use in connection with the land", thus when government aircraft flew over the chicken barn, causing the chickens to panic and fly against the inside of the barn killing themselves, the court found that the government had taken the air space (and presumably the chickens as well) by its direct and immediate interference with the use and enjoyment of the land). See also W. Blackstone, 2 Commentaries, §18, for the Latin legal maxim *Cujus est solum, ejus est usque ad coelum et ad infernos* or "To whomsoever the soil belongs, he owns also to the sky and to the depths".

[339] *United States v. Gerlach Livestock Co.*, 339 U.S. 725, 94 L.Ed. 1231, 70 S.Ct. 955 (1950); *Ball v. United States*, 1 Cl.Ct. 180 (1982).

property right which amounts to an actual physical invasion of the property. Not so obvious are cases in which takings have been found when there was less than a physical invasion. These cases are called "regulatory takings" or "inverse condemnations". The allegation is that the regulation has gone "too far" and so limited the use to which property may be put that the government might as well have condemned the property outright and taken all the badges of ownership including fee simple title.[340] These cases are called "inverse condemnations" because the plaintiff is the landowner whereas in ordinary condemnation cases the plaintiff is the government. The denial of a permit to develop a wetland has become a fertile ground for alleging a regulatory taking because the alternative functions of wetlands are so little understood and few other uses than development can be conceived for the land.

Assuming there is a property right which the law recognizes as protectable,[341] the next step is to focus on the character of the governmental activity to determine whether a regulatory taking has occurred. The first and most obvious is when the government actually invades the land, such as by building new roads, widening streets, erecting utility poles, and the like. The government will institute an action to force the landowner to sell his land for "just compensation". A middle type of case is when the governmental invasion is intermittent or less than continuous. In these cases the issue is the proper measure of damages.[342] The third and last type of governmental activity is when there is no physical invasion but a regulation is applied to limit the uses to which the property may be put. The essential inquiry in these "regulatory taking" cases

---

[340] *Deltona Corporation v. United States, supra.*

[341] Even this simple notion is complicated by the concept of a nuisance. Under the doctrine of nuisance, certain uses of land may be legitimately curtailed or eliminated if they impact negatively on natural resources such that the misuse of the resources injures the public. The legal maxim that "there is no property right in a nuisance" (*Sweet v. Rechel*, 159 U.S. 380, 40 L.Ed. 188, 16 S.Ct. 43 (1895; *Mugler v. Kansas*, 123 U.S. 623, 31 L.Ed. 205, 8 S.Ct. 273 (1887)) focusses on misuse of resources and allows governmental abatement of the misuse without there being any danger of a taking. Some environmentalists would extend this maxim to include land development in the concept of a nuisance because it destroys the function of wetlands to the detriment of the public interest in this resource.

[342] See e.g., *Ruckelshaus v. Monsanto, supra.*

will be whether it is fair to force a few private individuals to bear a burden alone (by not receiving any compensation for the limitation on the use of their property) or whether it is fair than the burden should be spread over all of society (by requiring the government to pay compensation out of the public fisc).[343]

The complaining landowner cannot stop a regulatory taking because the Taking Clause only prohibits uncompensated takings, not all takings.[344] There is no action available for injunction or declaratory relief when plaintiff alleges a taking. Instead, the landowner can only sue the government for compensation.[345]

In making a plaintiff's case, landowners should be aware that "there is no set formula to determine where a regulation ends and taking begins".[346] Concepts of fairness, justice, and judgment rule the day.[347] The Supreme Court has struggled to devise a system of analysis by which regulatory takings could be distinguished from abatements of nuisances (which have always been permissible under the police power of the government), minor intrusions on property ownership rights (without which government could not function), and major intrusions that amount to takings. Prior to 1922, the police power had been used to justify even some major intrusions.[348] The law

---

[343] *Agins v. City of Tiburon, supra*; *Penn Central Transportation Co. v. New York City, supra*.

[344] *First English Evangelical Lutheran Church v. County of Los Angeles, supra*; *Williamson County Planning Commission v. Hamilton Bank, supra*.

[345] The Tucker Act, 28 U.S.C. §1491, vests exclusive jurisdiction over taking cases in the United States Claims Court, unless the regulation or statute complained of states otherwise or requires other preconditions. However, even before going to the Claims Court, plaintiff must have exhausted all of his or her other administrative or state court avenues to compensation. *Williamson County Planning Commission v. Hamilton Bank, supra*.

[346] *Goldblatt v. Town of Hempstead*, 369 U.S. 590, 8 L.Ed.2d 130, 82 S.Ct. 987 (1962).

[347] *Andrus v. Allard*, 444 U.S. 51, 62 L.Ed.2d 210, 100 S.Ct. 318 (1979); *Penn Central Transportation Co. v. New York City*, 438 U.S. 104, 57 L.Ed.2d 631, 98 S.Ct. 2646 (1978).

[348] See e.g., *Mugler v. Kansas*, 123 U.S. 623, 31 L.Ed. 205, 8 S.Ct. 273 (1887) (holding that there is no taking if the government action involved preventing a detriment to the public, but there would be a taking if the government used the land to secure a benefit to the public); *Hadacheck v. Sebastien*, 239 U.S. 394, 60 L.Ed. 348, 36 S.Ct. 143 (1915) (holding that an ordinance outlawing

152

changed in 1922 with the *Pennsylvania Coal* case.[349] In that case a homeowner held an 1877 deed from a coal company which reserved the right to the coal company to remove coal from under the land. In 1921 Pennsylvania passed the Kohler Act which made mining coal illegal if it caused surface subsidence. The coal company argued that its coal had been taken by the passage of the Kohler Act and the majority of the Supreme Court agreed. *Pennsylvania Coal* stated a new test: the "diminution in value" test. Under this test, if a regulation goes "too far" and the diminution in value is consequently too great, there will be a taking. The dissent in *Pennsylvania Coal* was just as vigorous in arguing that mining coal which causes surface subsidence is a nuisance and can be legitimately eliminated by the police power. It may simply have been that the two opinions can be explained by their differing view of the facts: the majority believed that the subsidence would only affect the individual landowner thus if there was a nuisance it was not a public nuisance; the dissent believed that the mining subsidence would affect the entire city of Scranton and thus it was a public nuisance.

Another distinction between the majority and the dissent in *Pennsylvania Coal* centers on how to arithmetically determine the diminution in value, whether to value the property including both surface and mining rights, or to value the mining rights and surface rights separately. If valued together, even after forbidding mining, the land would retain some value, i.e., its surface value. If valued separately, the forbidding of mining would completely destroy the value of those property rights. If there is residual value, there is less diminution in value, but if there is no residual value, a greater diminution in value can be found. This debate continues today with wetland-permit-denied plaintiffs arguing that if they cannot develop their wetlands, then no value is left to them, while other say that even if the permit to develop is denied, the land may still be put to other uses thus retaining some value which prevents there being a taking.

After *Pennsylvania Coal* there was a 50-year hiatus in major taking cases until

---

brickyards, which utterly eliminated the value of Hadacheck's brickyard, was a legitimate exercise of the police power, even though the brickyard was not a nuisance).

[349] *Pennsylvania Coal Co. v. Mahon*, 260 U.S. 393, 67 L.Ed. 322, 43 S.Ct. 158 (1922).

Penn Central Transportation[350] and *Agins*.[351] *Penn Central* refined taking case analysis beyond the diminution in value test to include an examination of three factors: (1) the economic impact of the government action; (2) the extent to which there is interference with the distinct investment-backed expectations; and, (3) the character of the government action. Two years later another refinement came in *Agins* which was to be applied in land use cases: (1) does the regulation deny all economically viable use; and (2) does the regulation substantially advance a legitimate government interest? Wetland regulation is considered a land use question thus the *Agins* two-part analysis has been applied but the *Penn Central* three-part test is subsumed into the economic viability inquiry in the *Agins* test.

Under the substantial advancement test, the old concept of abating a nuisance arises as the court first looks to see whether the intended but now regulated use was a nuisance. If the court finds a nuisance, the case ends and there is no taking.[352] But if the court cannot find a nuisance, it must find some public benefit (a legitimate government interest) and then weigh the benefit against the burden to the landowner. In examining the burden to the landowner, the court moves to the three issues in *Penn Central*. A remaining economically viable use does not mean the property's highest and best use and is calculated including the value of the property as a whole.[353] Interference with investment-backed expectations analysis has been less than clear. Sometimes the courts

---

[350] *Penn Central Transportation Co. v. New York City, supra.*

[351] *Agins v. City of Tiburon, supra.*

[352] *Miller v. Schoene*, 276 U.S. 272, 72 L.Ed. 568, 48 S.Ct. 246 (1928).

[353] *Keystone Bituminous Coal Association v. DeBenedictis, supra.* (holding that a regulation requiring a coal company to leave half of its coal in place in order to support the surface was not a taking because the company could still sell the other half of its coal); *Penn Central Transportation Co. v. New York* City, *supra.* (holding that the denial of the use of the air space above Grand Central Station to build an office building was not a taking because the owner could still use the existing building). But see *Loveladies Harbor Inc. v. United States, supra.* (holding that the value of the remaining undeveloped eleven and one-half acres had been destroyed thus there was a taking although the original parcel was 250 acres); *Florida Rock Industries, Inc. v. United States, supra.* (holding that the denial of a permit to mine limestone on 98 acres of a 1,560-acre tract was a taking).

have found no interference when one would seem obvious.[354] The character of the governmental action inquiry distinguishes actual physical invasions from regulations on uses, and weighs the private burden against the public benefit or prevention of nuisances as previously discussed. Where there is a physical invasion, the diminution in value or interference with investment-backed expectations are irrelevant no matter how minor the invasion nor how great the public benefit obtained thereby.[355]

Analysis of taking cases still reveals a lightly applied set of criteria—some cases are orthodox applications, some are mysterious combinations in which some of the criteria are simply overlooked and others unnecessarily exalted, and others are simply aberrations. The future is even more murky when one considers the conflict between *Florida Rock*, and *Loveladies Harbor* and the great weight of previous authority which probably would not have found a taking in those cases. Executive Order 12630 only adds to the confusion.

In wetlands cases, arguments in favor of finding a taking by a permit denial center on the government's elimination of what has been viewed as the only use of otherwise useless land, i.e., development in a wetland. To accept this outcome, wetlands have to be conceived of as useless in their natural state and capable of economic viability only if they are developed. From a scientific outlook, such a concept is simply outdated. Wetlands do in fact have economic uses apart from their susceptibility to development. Arguments against finding a taking center on the nuisance exception in which a permit denial will always abate the nuisance of wetland destruction. This viewpoint is no longer practical given the public's ever-expanding demand for housing.

---

[354] *Andrus v. Allard, supra.* (holding that the ban on the sale of eagle feathers, which wiped out the value of plaintiff's stock of Indian artifacts, was held not a taking, even though plaintiff had originally purchased the artifacts before the ban for the sole purpose of reselling them).

[355] *Loretto v. Teleprompter Manhattan CATV Corp.*, 458 U.S. 419, 73 L.Ed.2d 868, 102 S.Ct. 3164 (1982) (holding that requiring a building owner to permit the attachment of cable television was a taking, albeit minor); *Kaiser Aetna v. United States*, 444 U.S. 164, 62 L.Ed.2d 332, 100 S.Ct. 383 (1979) (holding that the Corps' demand that a hitherto private pond be opened to the public was a taking).

Since the Clean Water Act is now over twenty years old, few real estate developers could reasonably hold an investment-backed expectation of profit from developing a wetland given the publicity and common knowledge attained by the §404 permit requirement. Likewise, development of wetlands is not always a nuisance given the recognition that some wetlands may be more valuable than others and the less valuable or already damaged may be developable without egregious harm to a public resource.

In the search for a guiding rule to analyze taking cases in wetlands development/permit denial cases, *Florida Rock* and *Loveladies Harbor* may contain the germ of a compromise. The property in both these cases was originally purchased before enactment of the Clean Water Act. It is reasonable to assume that those landowners at least started out with an investment-backed expectation of profit. However, with respect to property purchased after enactment of the Clean Water Act, it is difficult if not impossible to conceive of how an investment-backed expectation of profit could be reasonable. Certainly the landowner hopes he or she will get their §404 permit and make a profit, but they must also recognize that there is also a reasonable chance that their permit application will be denied. A hope is not a reasonable expectation. One recent case discussed the lack of a reasonable investment-backed expectation in profit in developing a wetland purchased after enactment of the Clean Water Act.[356] Perhaps an additional inquiry should be added at the very beginning of the court's analysis: when was the property purchased with the intent to develop it?

If it was purchased after the enactment of the Clean Water Act, then very careful inquiry should be made into the owner's actual expectations. To allow developers to purchase land, knowing there is a chance that a development permit will be denied, and then claim a Fifth Amendment taking when their permit application is denied, opens the door to collusive practices in which developers could guarantee themselves a profit, paid by the government, for any project plan, no matter how irrational, which would

---

[356] *Ciampitti v. United States*, 22 Cl.Ct. 310 (1991).

never receive a permit. At the same time, mitigation and wetlands-creation science and design should continue to expand, perhaps with some financial assistance from developers themselves, to ensure that a now-recognized vital resource is not needlessly destroyed to the detriment of a public resource, or excessively protected to the detriment of the public fisc.

TABLE OF AUTHORITIES

Cases

Statutes

Regulations

INDEX

GOVERNMENT INSTITUTES
MINI-CATALOG

PC #	ENVIRONMENTAL TITLES	Pub Date	Price
585	Book of Lists for Regulated Hazardous Substances, 8th Edition	1997	$79
4088	CFR Chemical Lists on CD ROM, 1997 Edition	1997	$125
4089	Chemical Data for Workplace Sampling & Analysis, Single User	1997	$125
512	Clean Water Handbook, 2nd Edition	1996	$89
581	EH&S Auditing Made Easy	1997	$79
587	E H & S CFR Training Requirements, 3rd Edition	1997	$89
4082	EMMI-Envl Monitoring Methods Index for Windows-Network	1997	$537
4082	EMMI-Envl Monitoring Methods Index for Windows-Single User	1997	$179
525	Environmental Audits, 7th Edition	1996	$79
548	Environmental Engineering and Science: An Introduction	1997	$79
578	Environmental Guide to the Internet, 3rd Edition	1997	$59
560	Environmental Law Handbook, 14th Edition	1997	$79
353	Environmental Regulatory Glossary, 6th Edition	1993	$79
625	Environmental Statutes, 1998 Edition	1998	$69
4098	Environmental Statutes Book/Disk Package, 1998 Edition	1997	$208
4994	Environmental Statutes on Disk for Windows-Network	1997	$405
4994	Environmental Statutes on Disk for Windows-Single User	1997	$139
570	Environmentalism at the Crossroads	1995	$39
536	ESAs Made Easy	1996	$59
515	Industrial Environmental Management: A Practical Approach	1996	$79
4078	IRIS Database-Network	1997	$1,485
4078	IRIS Database-Single User	1997	$495
510	ISO 14000: Understanding Environmental Standards	1996	$69
551	ISO 14001: An Executive Repoert	1996	$55
518	Lead Regulation Handbook	1996	$79
478	Principles of EH&S Management	1995	$69
554	Property Rights: Understanding Government Takings	1997	$79
582	Recycling & Waste Mgmt Guide to the Internet	1997	$49
603	Superfund Manual, 6th Edition	1997	$115
566	TSCA Handbook, 3rd Edition	1997	$95
534	Wetland Mitigation: Mitigation Banking and Other Strategies	1997	$75

PC #	SAFETY AND HEALTH TITLES	Pub Date	Price
547	Construction Safety Handbook	1996	$79
553	Cumulative Trauma Disorders	1997	$59
559	Forklift Safety	1997	$65
539	Fundamentals of Occupational Safety & Health	1996	$49
535	Making Sense of OSHA Compliance	1997	$59
563	Managing Change for Safety and Health Professionals	1997	$59
589	Managing Fatigue in Transportation, *ATA Conference*	1997	$75
4086	OSHA Technical Manual, Electronic Edition	1997	$99
598	Project Mgmt for E H & S Professionals	1997	$59
552	Safety & Health in Agriculture, Forestry and Fisheries	1997	$125
613	Safety & Health on the Internet, 2nd Edition	1998	$49
597	Safety Is A People Business	1997	$49
463	Safety Made Easy	1995	$49
590	Your Company Safety and Health Manual	1997	$79

Electronic Product available on CD-ROM or Floppy Disk

PLEASE CALL OUR CUSTOMER SERVICE DEPARTMENT AT (301) 921-2323 FOR A FREE PUBLICATIONS CATALOG.

Government Institutes
4 Research Place, Suite 200 • Rockville, MD 20850-3226
Tel. (301) 921-2323 • FAX (301) 921-0264
E mail: giinfo@govinst.com • Internet: http://www.govinst.com

AAO-4054

GOVERNMENT INSTITUTES ORDER FORM

4 Research Place, Suite 200 • Rockville, MD 20850-3226 • Tel (301) 921-2323 • Fax (301) 921-0264
Internet: *http://www.govinst.com* • E-mail: *giinfo@govinst.com*

3 EASY WAYS TO ORDER

1. Phone: **(301) 921-2323**
Have your credit card ready when you call.

2. Fax: **(301) 921-0264**
Fax this completed order form with your company purchase order or credit card information.

3. Mail: **Government Institutes**
4 Research Place, Suite 200
Rockville, MD 20850-3226
USA
Mail this completed order form with a check, company purchase order, or credit card information.

PAYMENT OPTIONS

❑ **Check** (*payable to Government Institutes in US dollars*)

❑ **Purchase Order** (this order form must be attached to your company P.O. <u>Note</u>: All International orders must be pre-paid.)

❑ **Credit Card** ❑ VISA ❑ MasterCard ❑ AMERICAN EXPRESS

Exp.___/____

Credit Card No. _____

Signature _____
Government Institutes' Federal I.D.# is 52-0994196

CUSTOMER INFORMATION

Ship To: (Please attach your Purchase Order)

Name: _____

GI Account# (*7 digits on mailing label*): _____

Company/Institution: _____

Address: _____
(please supply street address for UPS shipping)
_____

City: _____ State/Province: _____

Zip/Postal Code: _____ Country: _____

Tel: ( ) _____

Fax: ( ) _____

E-mail Address: _____

Bill To: (if different than ship to address)

Name: _____

Title/Position: _____

Company/Institution: _____

Address: _____
(please supply street address for UPS shipping)
_____

City: _____ State/Province: _____

Zip/Postal Code: _____ Country: _____

Tel: ( ) _____

Fax: ( ) _____

E-mail Address: _____

Qty.	Product Code	Title	Price

❑ **New Edition No Obligation Standing Order Program**

Please enroll me in this program for the products I have ordered. Government Institutes will notify me of new editions by sending me an invoice. I understand that there is no obligation to purchase the product. This invoice is simply my reminder that a new edition has been released.

15 DAY MONEY-BACK GUARANTEE

If you're not completely satisfied with any product, return it undamaged within 15 days for a full and immediate refund on the price of the product.

Subtotal_____
MD Residents add 5% Sales Tax_____
Shipping and Handling (see box below)_____
Total Payment Enclosed_____

Within U.S:	Outside U.S:
1-4 products: $6/product	Add $15 for each item (Airmail)
5 or more: $3/product	Add $10 for each item (Surface)

SOURCE CODE: BP01